God's Story—
and Ours!

First Church of the Brethren
1340 Forge Road
Carlisle, Pennsylvania 17013

God's Story—
and Ours!

Warren F. Groff

Foreword by Stanley Hauerwas

BRETHREN PRESS
Elgin, Illinois

God's Story—and Ours!

BRETHREN PRESS, 1451 Dundee Avenue,
Elgin, IL 60120.

Cover design by Kathy Kline

Previously published as *Story Time: God's Story and Ours* (Elgin, Ill.: Brethren Press, 1974)

Library of Congress Cataloging in Publication Data

Groff, Warren F.
 God's story—and ours!

 Rev. ed. of: Story time. 1974.
 Bibliography: p.
 1. Theology. 2. Story-telling (Christian theology)
3. Christian life—Church of the Brethren authors.
I. Groff, Warren F. Story time. II. Title.
BR118.G68 1986   248.4′865   86-20712
ISBN 0-87178-815-2

Manufactured in the United States of America

Contents

Foreword

God's Story and Ours is a wonderfully deceptive book. It
seems to be a book about the common things of life—an angry
word, an unspoken promise broken, an unanticipated compli-
ment, a youth fearing displeasing his or her parents—but in
fact it is a book about God. Yet the combination of the everyday and God accounts for the powerful effect this small book
has on the reader. Dr. Groff helps us see that nothing is more
significant than the common once we learn to view our lives
in terms of the God who has taken the time to be known in
and through the common.

There is perhaps no more difficult task than to write simply about what we all experience because on examination our
common experience turns out to have unanticipated depths
and complexities. Without burdening his text with extraneous
academic discussions about the nature of narrative, Dr. Groff
helps us to discover why the fact our knowledge of God comes
in a form of a story is crucial for helping us understand our
lives. Dr. Groff does not talk about doing narrative theology,
but rather he has shown us how illuminating theology can be
when God's story is confidently employed to portray our common life.

Moreover, this book is pastoral theology at its best. All
theology, when done well, is pastoral but few theologians today are able to combine theological rigor with the wisdom
necessary if theology is to inform our lives as Christians. For
wisdom deals with issues and judgments that are particular,
so one cannot rely on formulas or principles. To deal with

such matters you can only tell a story. That is precisely what Dr. Groff has done so well. He draws us into God's story by telling us stories with which we can identify, and thus discover the complexities of our own lives, our own personal story.

One other emphasis sets this book apart from many books currently being done in narrative theology. Dr. Groff emphasizes that it is not just stories that make Christians Christian, but the very definite story of God's presence in and through the life of Jesus Christ. Because that story is the unbreakable thread that God has woven into the very fabric of the universe, we discover in it the true story of our existence. This book, therefore, to be read rightly requires much of the reader. For to read this book well means we are invited to understand our lives in relation to God's story and in the process discover, like Augustine, that God has always been present in our lives. Such a discovery is of course as frightening as it is wonderful and we are indebted to Dr. Groff for helping us see that.

Stanley Hauerwas
The Divinity School
Duke University

1

"What's your point?"

WORDS and sentences are useful for describing things. But not only that. They also stop us dead in our tracks. They sneak up on us from behind. They say more, often less, than we intend. They tell a lot about us, and how we get along with others. They evoke memories that are unique to each person. They signal crossroads in human experience where conversation slows down and stops, where new discoveries startle us with their unexpectedness, where basic questions press in upon us.

What will tomorrow bring? Will we be strong, or will illness and death overtake us? Will we succeed in our cherished tasks? What will happen to those whom we care for and on whom we depend for life's meaning? Will we be able to solve the serious problems disturbing our nation and the world? Will there be another major depression? The future promises new possibilities, but it also threatens us with challenges.

Words and sentences become paragraphs. Paragraphs become stories. And stories bind things into larger wholes.[1] They shape our outlook on questions like the ones I just asked. The stories we tell in the home and in the church support a hopeful attitude. They help us cope with our anxieties about the future. They motivate us to act according to the values they promote. They put us in touch with ourselves, with our memories and feelings that define who we are.

The word story appears in some of our common expressions. The following examples illustrate how a story ties things together and invites a particular type of response. I occasionally find myself saying, "That's the story of my life!" I may be feeling sorry for myself because I have once again misjudged which would be the shorter check-out lane in the supermarket, or which drive-up window at the local bank would give me the faster service. Whether the misfortunes are this trivial or more serious, the point of the expression is the same. I am not only on the losing side in a given instance, but sense a long-term trend in that direction. A further implication is that others will agree with my self-assessment if they take the time to hear the "story of my life."

I was present at a church conference when a speaker was interpreting different facets of the church's worldwide program. Near the close of the session the speaker responded to a question by stating, "That's a different story!" We all knew what was meant. The question opened up another whole area for discussion. It would take considerable time to gather up the many interrelated factors bearing on the issue. An adequate answer would require a shift in our perspective. We would have to take up our position within an altered frame of reference. We needed to stand inside a "different story."

Some of our familiar hymns link the word story to the truth of the Gospel. Two suggest themselves immediately: "We've a Story to Tell to the Nations," and "I Love to Tell the Story." These hymns express the faith of the church that Jesus' story is—in a very special way—also God's story. They invite us to let God's story determine how we look on things, motivate what we do, and establish us as believers and disciples.

Throughout this book I suggest that we listen to the stories that play such an important part in the household and the church. The expressions I have framed in the chapter titles suggest times of questioning and discovery, of creative openness and dialog. Around them I propose to think with you about the assurances and uncertainties the conflicts and sought-after resolutions, the joys and sorrows of being human. Around them there are stories within stories just waiting for our discovering and being discovered by them. I shall only begin a process which awaits still other levels of completion. I assume very active participation by the reader who remains on center stage while I serve as a prompter from the wings.

Because of the everyday setting for the experiences and struggles that come into view, I deal with what is as familiar as life itself. But you may not have thought about these things quite in the way I present them, especially not in relation to biblical images, episodes, accents, and affirmations.

I often start a chapter with a story, a conversation, a sample litany that lets a particular situation leap out at you—I hope with the force of a "jack-in-the-box." Then we move back and forth through those intersections between individual experience, the practical wisdom we take for granted with others around us, and the larger story of God's purpose in Jesus Christ as that story unfolds in the Scriptures and in the church through its historical development.

The story of God's purpose unites "things in heaven and things on earth." Therefore, it belongs wherever things are happening that are most real to us. It is every bit as suitable in the kitchen and family room as in the parlor. Its story time is as relevant in the shop and political caucus as in Sunday morning worship.

Its meanings come alive where our struggles are most intense. I itemize the following as key intersections and special times for discovering and being discovered by God's story in relation to our own. They will figure preeminently in later chapters:

- the struggle to keep the promise we made (Chapter 2);
- the struggle for spontaneity and genuineness in personal relationships, the hunger for which is evident in the eagerness to ask and tell one another our names (Chapter 3);
- the struggle to belong, to be claimed by what is truly worthy of our loyalty, to begin again in the wake of failure, to sense a rightness that endures without pretending that things are better or worse than they are (Chapter 4);
- the struggle to be free, to be accountable to and for others while being oneself (Chapter 5);
- the struggle against illusion, against the lie that seems so believable and that keeps us from living in the "truth that sets us free" (Chapter 6);

• the struggle to grow, to survive, to be faithful to our convictions, while facing into the trouble that is inevitably part of life (Chapter 7);

• the struggle to accept the gift of gratitude, and to let that gratitude issue in deeds of loving service (Chapter 8);

• the struggle to live by the story we tell as the "story of our lives" (Chapter 9).

We reach toward what another person intends to say. Sometimes, a bit impatiently, we run ahead of what is actually being said. Almost from the first word the person speaks or writes, our minds pose the question: "What's your point?"

Hopefully, by these opening comments, I have begun to answer your mind's question. I have offered some clues about "what I'm driving at." I have foreshadowed the end toward which this book's unfolding story is pointed, the end which has been active from the beginning and which will be inviting your response along the way.[2]

2

"But you promised!"

PICTURE a middle-aged, somewhat sedentary father, comfortably lounging in his favorite easy chair. He's lost in—in whatever it is a person gets lost in when seated with eyes closed, half asleep, half awake. Just then his vigorous, sports-minded teenaged son stands in the doorway, baseball bat and glove in hand. Outside, some neighborhood youth have gathered, plus a few other reluctant fathers. The backyard, Sunday afternoon ball game is about to begin. The son has been trying for some minutes to arouse his lethargic father. Gentler persuasions have not succeeded. So the son finally penetrates the delicious semisleep with an intrusive: "Come on, Dad, they're all waiting! You promised!"

The father and son are on good terms, with strong ties of mutual affection and trust. The son knows that he will eventually dislodge his father from the chair and hold him to his word. Both of them sense that keeping a promise is very important![1] The father-son relationship, by definition, includes the imperative to share such activities as a Sunday afternoon, backyard ball game.

"Dad, you promised!"

"Yes, son, I know I did. Give me two more minutes."

The two minutes are needed to help the father find himself after being "lost in his thoughts"—usually a very pleasant lostness. The two minutes also assure the father that he will not be trapped in the labyrinthine passageways of his many obligations. After all, he has some rights and personal needs too.

What would life be like apart from the promises we make and struggle to keep? A son saying, "You promised!" to his father reminds us that to be a person is to exist in an intricate web of relationships. These relationships not only present us with deeply interior claims on our time and energy, but are fundamentally life-giving.

Looking back on my years as a growing child, I sense how impossible it would have been to "be" at all apart from being son of my parents, brother of two brothers—one older and one younger, grandson of grandparents, nephew of numerous uncles and aunts, and members of the Reinhart and Reba Groff household with neighbors who knew me in that particular context. It is equally clear that my adult selfhood is shaped by the fact that I am husband of a wife, father of a son, uncle to an enlarging tribe of nephews and nieces, and member of the Warren and Ruth Groff household with neighbors, colleagues, and friends who help me position myself within an extended family.

With these fundamental relationships come inward claims which keep asking for appropriate outward expressions. As a result, ceremonies and ritual language of all sorts spring up around them. At some time along the way you surely joined a childhood friend in pledging one another to secrecy with: "Cross your heart and hope to die." Whenever I participated in such an event, it was very serious business.

No doubt we all share a bit in society's superstitious, magical tendencies. Think of the continuing hold these taboos have: "Don't walk under the ladder." "Watch out for Friday the 13th." "Don't talk about things going well, or they'll turn bad." Ancient, darker feelings have a way of popping up just when we thought they had submerged forever.

But there are also more enlightened intuitions clustering around a "cross your heart" ceremonial. No matter how sophisticated we become we have an underlying awareness that promise-making has its solemnity and is deserving of fitting symbolic acts.

Explicit promises draw strength from, even as they give form to a whole complex of implicit imperatives and commitments. A man and woman enter into marriage. While they are not likely to say "cross my heart" to one another, other ritual words and behavior are very much in evidence: exchanging vows; gathering together friends and relatives; throwing rice, kissing the bride; decorating the getaway car.

You may not talk about these things on such joyful occasions, but think of the unfolding drama with its inevitable complications. What a tantalizing mixture of gladness and sadness, of ecstasy and struggle, for a man and woman to experience during a lifetime relationship. Few enter marriage thinking of the many unspoken claims and promises that go with the spoken: "I do." But who would care to miss the excitement of discovering and coping with those implied commitments to one another, to children, in-laws, grandchildren, and even great-grandchildren waiting in the wings?

"Where is she? My wife promised she would meet us on this corner at 5 o'clock sharp. I told her this car pool doesn't like to wait for anyone.

"Dad, you promised to be home by six so I could have the car."

"When did I promise that? I thought I told you I had to work late."

"I don't know how to tell them. I promised my family I wouldn't take business trips over weekends for awhile."

"Good news! We are about to become grandparents. Hope all goes well. Wonder if it will be a girl or a boy."

"Grandfather is getting so forgetful. Now that Grandmother is no longer living he can hardly stay alone much longer in that big house. Either we will have to take him in with us, or help get him established in a retirement home."

We could easily add to these vignettes. Many of our waking hours are spent in dealing with family concerns. And running through all these constitutive relationships are implicit claims on our attention and activity, as well as the explicit promises we made and try to keep.

Even as promises are the thread that holds the fabric of family life together, so they are the connecting tissues of an educational institution. I work in a seminary. We educate persons for ministerial service. We are organized like comparable schools: board of directors, president and administrative staff, faculty, students, standing committees, seminary council, president's advisory board, alumni association. There is an administrative chart showing lines of authority. There are also job descriptions for persons in charge of various parts of the program.

But these organizational arrangements are effective only as they are firmly rooted in the fertile soil of integrating claims and covenants that bind us together in an "on-purpose" venture. Faculty members promise to meet students in and out of class at designated times during the week. Students agree to complete assignments by certain deadlines. This level of promise-making is largely a matter of public record: class schedules, course syllabi, registration cards.

Around that formal core of any educational institution's activities there are numerous unspoken promises. Faculty members will reserve adequate time and energy to give their best to students. Even though they may be pulled equally in different directions at once, students are expected to establish priorities and to live by them. Administrative and support personnel are supposed to do all they can to provide the full range of learning resources essential for the program objectives. The comfort and general well-being of students and their families remain an institutional obligation. The president and board of directors are accountable to the supporting constituency and strive diligently to keep the institution faithful to its purposes as defined by the charter.

It would be easier if one implicit claim or explicit promise didn't have the nasty habit of getting in the way of another. A faculty person gets overcommitted to social causes—all of them worthy and in line with a highly principled conscience— only to have little time left for class preparation. A student finds it difficult to give adequate attention to studies without neglecting spouse and children. A seminary administrator has trouble maintaining academic freedom while also upholding values and standards the constituency wants to impose on the school.

How does one resolve conflicts as a promise-maker, whether as the member of a family or an educational institution? Some are easier to resolve than others. When you are the first to arrive at the scene of an automobile accident where persons are obviously injured, you will stop and give what aid you can even if you have to break a promise to get the family car home by a certain time.[2] If four or five other cars have arrived ahead of you, including the highway patrol, unless you are a physician you may well decide to get the car home.

Between these two relatively clear choices there are more difficult ones. Suppose you are the second car to arrive at an accident. The police are not there yet. It's not certain whether the passengers in the car ahead of you are better equipped to render first aid. Then the scales tip toward stopping, at least long enough to see if your help is needed. You might quickly discover that your best service is to continue on your journey, with the promise that you will call an ambulance and other service personnel as soon as you can.

What about a faculty person who struggles to balance involvements in larger social causes with daily class assignments? Such a person cannot expect to hold a teaching position for very long, with the commitments that position entails, unless adequate time is found for immediate instructional duties. And yet the broader interests are legitimate and important. So it takes judiciousness and courage to deal creatively with this tension.

Take the case of a student trying to be faithful to spouse and children and also to studies. Spouse and children have high priority. Studies may need to be postponed or at least prolonged. But where are the lines to be drawn? Might some of the family demands be unreasonable? What place should be made for the student's personal interest and vocational preferences? Don't they also warrant serious consideration? Isn't the concern for self-development intrinsically justifiable, even a duty among duties?

An efficient seminary administrator helps the institution manifest signs of health. Those signs include meticulous care in meeting obligations, with special attention to any interior claims that gather around a school's statement of its purposes as the basis for recruiting students and soliciting support. Also included are flexible structures for decision-making so that faculty, students, administration, and constituency stay in open dialogue with one another. Even then there will be conflict over particular policies and program directions. But in a well-functioning institution that conflict remains productive; it actually contributes to the vigor and adaptiveness of the whole enterprise.

This series of free-flowing thoughts about promise-making has hopefully reached the level of basic sentiments and dispositions. It has surfaced some key issues which warrant still sharper focusing. To accomplish that it will be helpful to summarize what has been emerging. Then we shall take note of biblical accents, themes, and stories that bear on our reflections.

Promise-making has its power from within an intricate network of family and larger institutional relationships which convey imperatives that are experienced directly "from the inside," and which press for suitable symbols and deeds that become visible "from the outside." Let's recall some illustrative cases which presented themselves to us during our earlier exposition.

A son's "You promised!" has its impact because to be father of a son presupposes readiness to share at deep levels, even to the point of being a reluctant participant in the ritualized behavior of a backyard ball game. Any father who is consistently inattentive to his son is an exception that proves the rule. Generous availability of the one to the other is the self-authenticating standard we use in judging such inattentiveness.

A teacher's disturbed conscience about lack of time for class preparation also witnesses to the way obligation may be felt "from the inside." In this instance the setting is an educational institution with greater complexity than the family. Any duly registered student has an immediate claim on the teacher and on the school whose announced purpose is to provide sound education for those who seek it.

We are often forced to decide between competing claims. Keeping a promise to get the car home by a specified time gets preempted by our stopping to give emergency aid to someone hurt in an automobile accident. Meeting pressing family needs interferes with one's schooling, which is being undertaken for enrichment of life through the cultivation of one's personal talents. Doing one's job as a teacher allows so little time for action projects designed to work toward constructive answers to broader community and national problems.

From the perspective of the Scriptures our life is nothing apart from the nourishing relationships within which we may grow, and from which we draw strength much as leaves do from branches, trunk, and roots. Those tacit claims we sense in the midst of our daily affairs are signals of a covenant that is meant to be written "on the heart" and not merely on "tablets of stone" (Jer. 31:31–34). To exist outside that foundational covenant (*berith* in the Hebrew) is sin and death. We are created for peace (*shalom*) which can be enjoyed only as righteousness (*tsedeqah*) prevails.[3] When such a healthy condition is experienced, then the privileges, as well as the rights and duties of each person, indeed of the whole creation, are honored. That's what the prophets had in mind when they called for justice to "roll down like waters, and righteousness like an ever-flowing stream" (Amos 5:24).

In what ways do these notions of covenant, peace, and righteousness help us cope with the competing claims we have been describing? I shall attempt an answer, but by way of a brief side trip into some varieties of ethical thought. Some ethicists approach this problem by use of the "utilitarian" criterion: if we decide to suspend one duty (promise-keeping, for example) in favor of another (giving emergency aid) that action must be justified by showing how it contributes more fully to the welfare of others. The goodness of a deed results from accurate discernment of what's best for the largest number of persons involved.

Others challenge this approach. They stress that duties

such as promise-keeping and giving emergency aid are oblig-
atory without any calculations about their comparative utility,
or their likely consequences. Ethical rules are more than sum-
maries of past experience. They are more than predictions
about future benefits based on previous results. They present
us with unqualified claims. Thus if one duty needs to be suspended because another conflicts with it, the resultant action
represents an exception to a rule. And ways have to be found
to support the rule even though it is temporarily suspended
since it gives form to a basic presupposition, a fundamental
structure, of life in its depth. The rightness of an action
results from its conformity to duty.[4]

The biblical writers rarely engaged in this type of ethical
reasoning.[5] And yet if one had to place the Scriptures on one
side or the other of this debate, the primary accent would be
on the second position. The theme of covenantal wholeness
includes strong emphasis upon disciplines, laws, or marks of
blessedness which are understood to be indispensable to that
wholeness. Some of these markings are stated succinctly in
the Ten Commandments (Ex. 20:1-17) and in the Beatitudes
(Matt. 5:3-12).[6] They give the road map for the pilgrim people of ancient Israel and all their successors. They point the
way toward the rightly ordered, the straight, or the normal life
of peace and righteousness.

The Scriptures are not necessarily hostile to a principle
like the "greatest good for the largest number" to guide our
decisions among rival bids for our concern and investment. In
its own fashion that principle is also reaching toward fundamental justice for all. But we must not overlook the distinctiveness of biblical tendencies. The distinctiveness revolves
around the clear insistence that right neighbor-relationships
are qualified by the need for a right God–relationship.

The Ten Commandments are about equally divided between orientations—toward God: no apostasy, idolatry, blas-
phemy, or irreverence; and toward the neighbor: no
dishonoring of parents, murdering, stealing, bearing false witness, or coveting what is not one's own. Stated positively, it is
the sturdy, justice-filled love of God and neighbor that brings
order (mishpat) into the multiplicity of relationships and
claims. Whether a particular act is good or right is deter-

mined at the deepest level in terms of its fittingness in light of God's prior purpose and action.

The fitting response often involves startling expansions or reversals of meaning.[7] Doesn't common sense dictate that we dare not become so global in our promise-making that we find ourselves unable to be promise-keepers at all? For then we fall victim to such seductive thoughts as these: "Reach for that more distant promise and find an excuse to hedge on those immediate, pressing obligations that reflect the actual contours of your place and time. Put no limits on your commitments. Promise more than you can deliver for then you can't be blamed if you fail."

The Scriptures support us in admitting our finiteness. It is God alone who says Yes to some things without at the same time being required to say No to others. We are required to say No to many other possible investments and commitments in order to say Yes to some and really mean it.

But biblical writers never dwell long on the dangers of overextending our promises, or on the limitations that gather around our finiteness. The strongest accent is on the threat of provincialism, of downright stinginess in the giving of ourselves on behalf of the neighbor. Cautions like these seem so very reasonable: "Don't overextend yourself. Keep your promises close to the vest. Play it safe. You have already made more promises than you can keep. If you don't look out for your own interests and those of your immediate family, who will?"

In the face of such self-protectiveness, the meaning and identity of the neighbor have been redefined by the life and ministry of Jesus. Blood relationships and physical proximity are not allowed to limit or define those who can lay claim to our personal strengths and resources. Everyone in need, whether near or far, becomes the locus of our accountability; and the one who responds appropriately demonstrates what it truly means to be a neighbor (Luke 10:29–37). So drastic is the reorientation required of us that even the enemy is to be included in our immediate circle of care and responsibility. "Love your enemies and pray for those who persecute you. . . . For if you love those who love you, what reward have you? . . . And if you salute only your brother, what more are you doing than others?" (Matt. 5:43–48)

God's prior election of Israel is the model for this outgoing, barrier-breaking love. One sensitive writer after another reminded the Israelites that God's concentration of his covenant intentions on them is for the sake of the whole human community. The particularity of love does not necessarily imply parental favoritism. If anything, the God of Abraham, Isaac, and Jacob is always partial to the ones left out of the circle: homeless strangers, poor people, widows, orphans, captives. After all, hadn't the Israelites themselves been delivered from slavery in Egypt, allowed to pass through the waters of the Red Sea unscathed, given a land of promise, and pulled back repeatedly from the brink of extinction as a people?

The most radical challenge to common sense is the biblical imperative that we trust God so implicitly that we become like a little child who is willing to jump from a high place into the waiting father's arms simply upon the command to do so. Recall how Abraham was asked to sacrifice his only son, Isaac, born late in the lifetime of Abraham and Sarah, long after the time for such things (Gen. 22:1–19). If Abraham obeyed, how could God possibly keep his promise to make him the father of the covenant people, and give him descendants as numerous as the grains of sand on the seashore? Given her old age, Sarah wasn't likely to conceive again.

We are to trust God with childlike simplicity and directness. That is what disciplines all our promise-making. That is the reliable compass which charts our course through life's many relationships and competing claims. It may set "a man against his father, and a daughter against her mother, and a daughter-in-law against her mother-in-law; and a man's foes will be those of his own household" (Matt. 10:35–36). But even when it becomes a sword to divide us from family and friends, that childlike trust in God has the simplifying, centering, anxiety-freeing impact of what Jesus taught: "Seek first his kingdom and his righteousness, and all these things will be yours as well" (Matt. 6:33).

Jesus lived what he taught. In his life we have been given the saving image of unqualified simplicity and trust. In his obedience, which led to death on the cross, we meet the graciousness of God that turns all our familiar meanings on their head: *by losing our life we find it; in the midst of death we live.* God has the habit of renewing his promise most dramatically just when it seems impossible to keep. Abraham was asked to "give up" his son even though he could scarcely expect to receive the promised descendants without Isaac. Jesus faced the agonizing threat of death, and went to the cross supported only by his faith that God's covenant promise would still be kept on the other side of the grave.

And it was! So now we have it on the authority of Christ's own resurrection. An open invitation has been extended without any strings attached. We may trust God's invincible trustworthiness. His promise is the very same power apart from which we would not be at all. His is the power that makes for health, that gives renewal in the face of our betrayals. Even an earthly father will scarcely give his son a stone when he asks for bread. Why, then, do we expect so little of the heavenly father? We may lean against him with the urgency of a teenaged son confronting his father: "You promised!"

The substance and the style of the invitation make it clear that God does not even ask for two minutes. God keeps the promises he makes, even before we remind him.

3

"What's your name?"

SHE STOOD less than three feet tall, age two, going on three. Easter was still several months away. It was not even Sunday. But there she was, her hair carefully braided and ribboned, a daintiness to her fluffy blue dress. She had more of a party-going than a Saturday-morning-shopping look about her.

A casually dressed woman stood beside her, presumably the little girl's mother. She was in the store to pick up electrical supplies just as I was. Two other women arrived while I was waiting for my purchases to be billed and wrapped. The three of them were obviously old friends. Even if I had tried, I couldn't have helped overhearing the conversation that began immediately.

Attention quickly turned to the little girl. How grown up, how pretty she looked! Then the overtures took a familiar turn: "What's your name? Come on, tell us. Bet you don't know it." They already knew her name. The little girl knew they knew it. But they were still asking her as I walked out the door. I wish I could have stayed to hear her tell it.

"What's your name?" behaves a lot like "Hello!" or "Hi!" It can be as perfunctory as any such greeting. But not when it's pursued with all the earnestness of our opening litany. Then the question signals an important happening, a time of hopefulness, when promise-filled relationships are just waiting to be delivered.

There's something truly satisfying about receiving the gift of a person's name. And it is a gift. We can invite. We can urge: "Come on, tell us." But we cannot demand. At least it's not the same if a person is forced to tell. Then something priceless is lost. Both the person doing the forcing and the one being forced are violated.

I take extra precautions to keep my credit cards from being stolen. For if they are stolen, the thief really steals my name. I've been forced to tell. A credit card is an extension of my promise-making capacities. The card carries my signature which, when used properly, validates the promises I make. A good credit rating depends on keeping my commitments to pay by a certain date. So the thief takes more than a piece of plastic. It's my personal integrity that's at stake and not simply the threat of receiving bills for goods and services I didn't receive.

Name-telling should be a deeply personal interchange. It is to be entered into as an act of mutuality and expectancy for the enrichment of life itself. Whoever steals my credit card, then, takes something of my very personhood. That individual suffers the person-destroying effects of pretending to be someone else, literally of living off a borrowed identity. No person should fall victim to the illusion that name-telling is a commodity one can exploit for selfish advantage. Any such distortion invades my life as well, not only in my relationship with the thief, but with all who mistakenly think they are dealing with me.

Name-dropping also preys upon spontaneity in human relationships. The one whose name is dropped is not usually consulted. So that person's freedom and integrity are embezzled. We cry out against guilt-by-association. But advertising permanently bonds images of famous athletes and television stars to particular products and thus motivates us to buy. It is an attempt at virtue-by-association and, at its worst, exploits the power of a name.

Surely you have answered your telephone and been greeted by someone who uses your name with great familiarity. The tone of voice is meant to imply that you have known each other for life. Minutes into the conversation you realize you are receiving a sales-pitch for land in Arizona or some other product.

Early in our marriage my wife and I lived in New Haven, Connecticut. I was taking graduate study. Ruth was managing two jobs to help make the dollars stretch far enough. We had a second-floor apartment. Our name card was posted by the bell at the foot of the outside stairway. The school I attended was large. So the crew-cut young man—that was before hair styles changed—who rang the bell one day could easily have been a classmate whose name I'd forgotten. At least his "Hi, Warren!" made me think so. I invited him up the stairs, almost falling over myself in my haste to usher him into our apartment. He wasn't a fellow student. Before I knew it, I had subscribed to a magazine we didn't need and couldn't afford.

Whoever wrenches our name from us, either by fiat or subterfuge, exerts power over us. We aren't invited to disclose ourselves as participants in mutual sharing and growing relationships. Our name, our very person, is reduced to an object and pushed around. We are rendered vulnerable, and not with the voluntary vulnerability that goes with spontaneity in name-telling.

Forced vulnerability threatens and angers us. That anger may smolder under the politeness we struggle to maintain. But it's there. We experience it when exploited. Others do too if we encroach upon their cherished freedom.

Family names originated for many reasons, some circumstantial. Being someone's son: *Johnson*. Living in a certain place: *Underhill*. Belonging to one of the trade guilds: *Smith, Baker, Meyer* (farmer), *Kaufman* (storeman), *Miller, Bowman*. Having particular skills: *Singer*. Reflecting physical traits: *Stout, Short, Strong, Long*.

In selecting first names parents have taken their inspiration from many sources: national heroes, political leaders prominent at the time, colorful entertainment personalities, close relatives—I was named after an uncle (Warren) and a grandparent (Frederick), religious history. The Bible remains a basic source—my wife's name is Ruth Naomi and our son's is David. Some societies nowadays publish an approved list from which to select, in order to protect the child from a name that will be a constant source of embarrassment.

However accidental their origins, both given and family names become far more than playthings to be bandied about in jest. At any age we are understandably hurt if that abuse occurs. I enjoy seeing my name in print, and I much prefer that it be spelled correctly. I want people to remember me. Although it happens, I dislike being taken for someone else. It's not difficult to understand why. Just think how often we respond to the identity-forming, relationship-building question: "What's your name?" Our repeated responses keep strengthening an awareness of who we are, and from way down inside.

Contemporary prisoners of war have undergone brain-washing (today's version of the thumbscrew and torture rack) at the hands of captors who wanted to extract information or some confession from them. They tell of their intense struggles to repeat their name—to themselves, their jailors, the walls if nothing else—as they teetered on the abyss of insanity, total forgetfulness, or the lost of personal awareness that is tantamount to death.

When we identify ourselves, or others call us by name, there is evoked a sense of somehow being the same and yet different as we recall the years that have passed. Preschool, adolescent, adult—each stage of maturation brings its distinctive feelings, struggles, defeats, victories. But each later stage blurs into and catches up memories of how we felt and some of the things that happened along the way. The past leaves its markings upon us, biologically, and as developing persons not only with promise-making but also name-telling capacities. The future is also there, for our anticipations mingle closely with memories and commitments.

You have your own life with its recollections and dreams, and I have mine. No matter how well we might learn to know each other, there will always be privacy and irreducible distinctiveness. Being asked and telling one's name brings self-knowledge that has a quality all its own.

And yet we do get to know each other in ways that are comparable to knowing ourselves.[1] Another person's name also solicits a feeling of continuity through change, of sameness through difference, as we think of the interchanges we have had from the moment of meeting and over a period of time. Haven't you run into an old friend, even after many years of separation, and picked up almost where you left off? Getting married, having children, becoming grandparent, changing jobs, losing some hair, gaining weight, turning gray—any number of things may be different. But it's the same person.

I came home recently from a conference, and told my wife about meeting a friend neither of us had seen for over ten years. She wanted all the news about him: if he had changed much, whether his wife was along, where they lived and worked, how old their son is now, what we talked about. Simply mentioning his name brought back a flood of memories to my wife. I could tell by the questioning that her relationships with the friend and his family had picked up as easily as my own. Being apart one day, six months, ten years, does make a difference; and yet personal friendships leap across such hurdles with remarkable agility.

A person's name is so much more than a coat to be put on and off. This observation will have more force if we note differences in the way words perform in our conversations. Some words, singly or in phrases and sentences, give us information. They help us know what a thing is like. How big it is. How it works. What its distinguishing traits are. While shopping for a new car we may be told: "That model has a longer wheelbase, for a more comfortable ride. It comes with a four-barrel carburetor. But it still operates efficiently on regular gasoline."

Traffic signs also give straightforward, no-nonsense instructions. Quick action is expected: CURVE AHEAD. SLOW DOWN. ONE WAY. NO OUTLET.

Words that give us information or instructions are direct. No shadowy edges surround their central meaning to stimulate the creative imagination, at least not if they are clearly stated and understood as intended. But not all words serve the same way. If some focus attention outward by telling us what things are like and what to do, others direct us inward and feature our relationship to external objects and possible courses of action. These are image-evoking. They draw from us a sense of participation in a living whole, much like the flag symbolizes our belonging to the nation.

In this instance, through a long process of social development, the flag is not merely an external object being described, but an internal network of relationships, identifications, loyalties, assurances, and aspirations being experienced. The symbol (flag) and what it symbolizes (nation) may be so closely wedded in our sentiments and dispositions that discourtesy to the one implies the same to the other. Even those who abuse the flag, perhaps as part of anti-war protests, presuppose the connection. Otherwise, their act would have no power.

A strong example of an image-evoking word, or symbol, is a person's name.[2] When we think of some person we know, there are descriptive details that come to mind: age, weight, height, color of hair and eyes, sex. But the name conveys so much more than objective data of this sort. The name evokes the *presence* of the whole person: memories, life-happenings, predictable character traits, affectional ties, shared associations.

It is time now to summarize the thoughts that have flowed so far from our lead question: "What's your name?"

Being asked and telling our name helps develop a basic awareness of who we are. That kind of interchange is meant to be an intensely personal act of mutual sharing and accountability.

Name-telling is an important facet of promise-making. Our signatures validate the promises we make.

Personal relationships are not a commodity to be exploited for selfish gain. To believe otherwise is to be victimized by a lie.

Whoever misappropriates our name, by stealing credit cards, check-forging, or pressure tactics to sell products, exerts power over us, and renders us vulnerable in a way that embezzles our freedom and integrity. If we do the same to others we contribute to the degenerative disorders that infect humanity.

Words may offer information and give instruction, or they may be image-evoking. A person's name is a clear example of the latter. The symbol (name) and the reality (person) become so closely identified that one directly implies, and calls forth the *presence* of the other in our memories and anticipations.

These reflections keep us standing at a busy crossroad. A great many episodes and themes from the Judeo-Christian story keep whizzing by. It's difficult to know which to flag down and which to wave on. I shall only feature several, with brief editorial comments and affirmations along the way.

(1) Adam helped to name the original inhabitants of that ancient, unspoiled garden, and thus shared in God's own power and creativity (Gen. 2:19–20).

To name someone, not superficially but at the level of what one is really intended to be, is to call that one into being. The power to name is the power of life itself. That's frightening, especially if we think of the way it works in the society we have all helped to shape. We come equipped with interior potentialities, but are dependent upon forces outside ourselves for their actualization. We do not mature apart from what the environment and other persons contribute to our formation. And this maturation does not take place without struggle or without facing built-in requirements for personal growth.

Take those reared in ghettoes, with inadequate food, housing, education, and health care. They are named second-class citizens by circumstances and entrenched social patterns that communicate more powerfully than words. All others who fight to maintain their first-class status and privileges contribute to this downgrading. Those trapped in the ghettoes may even acquiesce and perceive themselves as inferior. But not without anger. Both the oppressor and the oppressed suffer from these disordered systems and relationships, like a credit card thief is victimized along with the victims.

God's naming cuts clean and keeps probing for that integrity toward which the whole creation points. God's calling forth of life has firmness and liveliness. He judges all counterproductive behavior. He offers the only sure prescription for health. He is the only adequate foundation for hope that endures in spite of what often seems so hopeless.

(2) Adam saw Eve in that garden lineup at the dawn of life, and came to new self-awareness by encountering one with whom he sensed a strange affinity, yet who was deliciously

different: "That at last is bone of my bones and flesh of my flesh . . ." (Gen. 2:23). Man and woman, male and female in God's good creation are so capable of contributing to the fulfillment of each other. Anticipation and promise were there in Adam's glint of knowing recognition as he spotted Eve: "Yeah! I like that one! The best I've seen so far!" It was mingled with agony yet to come, but ecstasy were there, nevertheless.

We stand under Adam's mandate to contribute to an ongoing person-forming process. You speak my name and I speak yours. I speak your name and you speak mine. In that litany of co-creation God's power in naming extends itself into our daily affairs.

(3) One biblical personality after another underwent a name change, and thus was positioned within the integrating story line of God's covenant purpose.

Abram, exalted father, became Abraham, father of a multitude (Gen. 17:5). Jacob, who cheated Isaac out of his birthright and deceived many others as well, became Israel, the representative of the called-out people (Gen. 32:28). Simon, vacillating, timid, became Peter, the rock (John 1:42). Saul, Pharisee and persecutor of the Christians, became Paul, servant of the crucified-risen Christ (Acts 13:9).

The American Indians often assigned names to match actual accomplishments as persons matured. James Fenimore Cooper was well aware of this when he had Natty Bumppo called Deerslayer, in the novel of that name, to mark his status as hunter. Later he had him dubbed Hawkeye by a fallen Indian who acknowledged he was dying at the hands of a distinguished warrior.

Biblical characters were not usually feted for their attainments. However, they were assigned new names to foreshadow new beginnings. Saul became Paul at the time of his conversion, anticipating his exploits as the apostle to the Gentile world. The new name catches up the promise of what one is becoming, not through one's prowess but through God's ingenuity and strength. How else could Jacob, with all his craftiness, be named Israel, the very epitome of the covenant people? How else could Simon be named Peter, the rock, capable as he was of denying his Master three times even after he had been warned? The covenant has an outcome that is much surer than the achievements of those persons who are its earthen vessels. A good thing, or it's not likely that God would ever reach his own goals for his creation.

(4) Moses encountered God before a burning bush that was not consumed, asked him, "What's your name?" and God told him, "I am who I am" (Ex. 3:1–22).

Can it be that Moses really didn't know God's name? Or was it more like asking a little girl in a fluffy blue dress to tell us what we know already, but want to receive as a free gift, as an enriching presence, as the basis for a deepening relationship?

Whatever else, Moses knew that things weren't going too well. His people, heirs of the covenant promise, were a ragamuffin band of exiles in Egypt. Joseph had been forgotten. Forced labor was everywhere. Moses had led a slave revolt that fizzled. Rumor had it that he killed a man. He had fled for his life, and was hiding in the desert with some relatives.

Moses needed a renewed relationship with the God of Abraham, Isaac, Jacob, and Joseph. Even the spectacular meeting on the mountain, and God's initial assurance, were not enough to overcome Moses' reluctance to assume the leadership role requested of him. He asked for more and got it. God volunteered his name, and thus ventured, risked, humbled himself before one of his creatures who was hotheaded, stubborn, and known to stray from the straight and narrow.

In so doing God sealed his promises with his own name. Freely transliterated, he was saying to Moses: "Does the future seem threatening? It need not be. Address the silence with confidence. Someone's there whose name you know. *I will be what I will be*, before you, beside you, behind you. Abandon yourself to the firmness of my loving purpose which will never let you down."

(5)What more could anyone ask? But ask they did, as the story unfolds, until the form of the asking and God's telling were permanently altered in the "fullness of time."

Jesus Christ elected not to stay aloof by laying claim to heavenly rank, but emptied himself, became freely vulnerable, took "the form of a servant, being born in the likeness of men . . . obedient unto death, even death on a cross" (Phil. 2:5-8).

Since "God has highly exalted him"—

—Jesus Christ is "the name which is above every name" (Phil. 2:9);

—Jesus Christ is the name, the personalized signature, that validates the covenant, for "all the promises of God find their Yes in him" (2 Cor. 1:19-20);

—Jesus Christ is the name that embodies the *presence* of God in all his "glory and truth; we have beheld his glory, glory as of the only Son from the Father" (John 1:14);

—Jesus Christ is the name given with God's own spontaneity, and thus with the freedom and integrity toward which the promise-filled future draws us all.[3]

"What's your name? Come on, tell us. Bet you don't know it." God knows his name. He knows that we know it. But let's all stay around and rejoice in the telling.

4

"Just because!"

LET's eavesdrop on a son in vigorous debate with his mother:
"Why can't I sleep out tonight?"
"A storm is threatening. Didn't you hear the weather forecast?"
"But it's not raining now. Why can't I?"
"You'll get wet. You're already sneezing around the place. You'll catch cold for sure."
"We'll stay in the tent. Besides it's brand-new."
"You'll be afraid when the storm comes. You know you don't like thunder and lightning. You'll come running into the house and disturb us all."
"Gee, Tommy says he can, if I can. Why can't I?"
"Just because! That's why."

Listen next to a wife trying to cope with a persistent husband and son:
"Why don't you want to sleep overnight along the lake? The tent is new and the air mattresses comfortable. That way we can fish for bass late at night and early in the morning."
"The mosquitoes will eat me alive. They almost did last year."
"We'll buy hats with netting. They'll help. You'll like it."
"I wouldn't sleep at all. You know the lake borders on a swampy marsh. Think of the noises: frogs, crickets, beavers slapping their tails, even wolves howling. No thanks."

"We'll be there to protect you. Come on, join us. Why not?"

"Just because! That's why. Just because!"

———

In this third exchange a son is defending his musical tastes before an equally opinionated father:

"Why don't you like Emerson, Lake, and Palmer? It's a creative group. Listening would be even better if we had a 4-channel system."

"Oh, they're all right. But must you play your records so loud? I get a headache."

"Music is to be felt, not just heard with ears."

"Perhaps, but must the rafters shake? How can you lie there right in front of the speakers? You'll be deaf before you're twenty. Why do you like to play it so loud?"

"Just because! It's great. Only way to listen to music."

———

When "just because" intrudes itself during such household litanies, the conversation stops but is hardly ended.

Usually there is impatience. Something is so clear to one, it is inconceivable that another person might fail to see it.

The temptation is verbal dogmatism. Just because I say so, that's why. That's just the way it is.

No step-by-step argument is likely to help the one who doesn't see, for factors predisposing the one who does see are so total, so interior and cozy they are simply taken for granted.

It's not whether someone sees this or that item clearly. And more's involved than making adjustments for those who hold things close or far away, as I must, to get a better view. How we see all that we see—that's what is at stake.[1] Do we have eyes to see, not by birth necessarily, but by rebirth, by conversion to a particular way of seeing things: fishing, tenting, physical comfort, welfare of children, order in the household, loud music?

In all this talk about seeing and having eyes to see, I've been using vision as an inclusive metaphor, and investing it with specialized meanings. It catches up how we think and feel about this or that. The way we see affects what we like and dislike. And there's little point in pretending. We may hope eventually to like something, even fighting mosquitoes for the sake of fishing, but if we don't like it now, that's just the way it is. It's the same with other preemptive feelings: anger, boredom, embarrassment, anxiety, contentment. They "just are."

"Just because!" flags a total response, a whole bundle of sentiments and dispositions shaped by a vision of what's true. This reference to truth, in the setting of comments about "just because" situations, leads directly into some accents from the Gospel of John.

Truth is not simply accurate statements about things, although those are always worth their weight in gold. For John's Gospel, truth is the light by which we see, bright as the sun, the source of creative energy, the charter and goal of our deepest feelings and aptest investments.

Jesus Christ is the way, the truth, and the life; the truth that sets us free, the truth that is a light driving out the menacing darkness, the truth by which we see all that is to be seen, for it is the light of the world.

John describes one time after another when it was very difficult for persons to get the point, to see what Jesus was driving at: A Samaritan woman at the well thought Jesus meant the water that quenches physical thirst rather than water that satisfies deep spiritual needs (John 4:1–12). Jews responded to Jesus' assurances about the truth that will set them free by saying they were descendants of Abraham and had never been in bondage to anyone (John 8:31–33). Nicodemus greeted Jesus' reference to the need to be born again—if one is to see the kingdom of God—with skepticism about the feasibility of going through the birth process a second time (John 3:1–4).

These are crossroads where meaning pass one another like ships in the night, where there is One who "sees" and many who do not, where all the lights are on in the house, yet people stumble around as though they are in the dark. John describes "just because" situations right and left.

Why was it so hard for the Samaritan woman, the Jews, Nicodemus, and others to "see" what Jesus had in mind? We have a decided advantage. The Gospel of John, the Scriptures as a whole, the teachings of the church—all give us clues about what's going on. And yet, how very easy for us also to stumble around in the dark although the lights are on.

I believe Jesus Christ is the very name of God, the one who firmly establishes God's presence in human affairs, and discloses God's trustworthiness as a promise-keeper. If you were to ask me to state my faith in one sentence, that would be my affirmation. It draws upon language used by Paul during an intense interchange with the church in Corinth. While assuring his critics that their word had not been an ambiguous blend of Yes and No, he said: "For the Son of God, Jesus Christ, whom we preached among you, Silvanus and Timothy and I, was not Yes and No; but in him it is always Yes. For all the promises of God find their Yes in him" (2 Cor. 1:19,20). Or, to give a free translation, he is the signature validating all of God's promises.

I find it difficult to give step-by-step reasons why I believe that. But I can describe my own pilgrimage as one way of giving an accounting of the faith by which I live. I do so out of the conviction that Jesus Christ is the clearest title the church has for its outward-reaching story, its "good news." Not only the lives presented in the Scriptures, but your life and mine, indeed all living things, are caught up in that story line which centers in him and which holds it all together. I trust that my personal recital will encourage you to think of suitable ways to render an accounting of the faith and hope you have been given in Christ.[2]

I grew up close to the town of Harleysville, Pennsylvania. Many of my immediate relatives on my father's side have lived there for generations. My mother still does. When I arrived on the scene in 1924 the area was largely agricultural. Some of the farmers retailed their products in Philadelphia and nearby suburbs. I know, because I helped when I was in the teens.

The dialect known as Pennsylvania Dutch was prevalent. I heard it about as much as English. I don't know why I never learned to speak it better than I did, although I came to understand it well enough to get the drift of those conversations which suddenly shifted to the dialect in the hope that youthful ears might not catch what was being said.

A high percentage of the people were churchgoers. Different denominations were represented, but many were either Mennonites or members of the Church of the Brethren. I had strong roots in both, but heard more plain-garbed Mennonite preachers in the early years. The Church of the Brethren finally won out when my parents were installed as deacon and deaconess.

Until I was eight going on nine, we lived within walking distance of a one-room school. I began first grade at age five. There were only eighteen students altogether, so the teacher agreed to take me a year early. It's as though I were still there: slanted, hinged-top desks, with ink wells and fascinating doodles pressed into the surfaces by students who pretended they were practicing penmanship on their copy pads; recess signaled by a bell in the steeple; potbellied stove in the corner; teacher's desk, blackboard, and flag in the front of the room; tin lunch boxes, colorfully painted, and small thermos bottles held firm by swinging fasteners inside; smells of bananas and oranges and other things; fresh water from a hand-dug well drawn up by a metal pump handle that squeaked; double doors in the front that were usually wide enough except the day one of my front teeth was chipped during a fight— obviously he was older and much bigger.

They boarded up the building just as I was beginning fourth grade. We traveled by bus to the new consolidated school in town—four rooms instead of one, central heating, inside plumbing, new desks with smooth but less interesting tops, a marvelous ball diamond outside. It was exciting. I learned a lot. But something had passed—indeed was passing in many communities as school consolidation swept the country. It would be several decades before the idea of "ungraded, free" groupings of student and "learning centers" would emerge with the novelty of a brand-new thought and highlight some of the values I experienced in one room with all grades, learning from the total environment at my own speed.

Home, church, school, town—all contributed to my growth. I was given direct, accurate, sometimes irritating, information about things that were part of my everyday world.

That's a spoon. Eat with it. That's a door mat. Wipe your feet
on it. That's a baby brother. Don't hit it. That's a church pew
(hard and straight). Don't squirm on it. That's a chicken
house. Keep it clean. (We had enough chickens for a chicken
farm, so I was carefully briefed on this point.) That's a car.
Drive it carefully.

I was given enduring memories and associations in the
midst of all this instruction. One item from that everyday
world of things, persons, and relationships snuggled up to
another with the image-evoking power that motivates and stirs
at deep levels.

I told you about persons in my home community speaking Pennsylvania Dutch. Inked into my mind with grooves as
deep as those on the slanted desk tops are some highly descriptive words, usually spoken as part of strong admonitions.

Bist net so Doppich. You're so awkward. There you go,
falling all over yourself, always dropping things.

Bist net so Rutschlich. You squirm too much. Sit still.

Bist net so Wunnerfitslich. You're too nosy. You pry into
things you shouldn't.

Du bist ein kleine Schnickelfritz. That expression still
evokes feeling of warmth and approval, of being OK.

Remembered associations from which I continue to draw
strength not only include such family words but also activities. Take our annual fishing week in the Poconos, even during post-depression years, catching pickerel we didn't enjoy
eating let alone cleaning, sleeping on makeshift beds, doing
without electricity, rowing a boat until our arms ached, having
breakdowns on roads too steep and rough for cars of 1930–40
vintage. So powerful are the shaping memories of family sharing during these times that I try to repeat the past each summer as Ruth, David, and I, usually with other friends, endure
similar inconveniences while on our yearly fishing pilgrimage
to Canada.

I can never remember a time when Jesus Christ was ab-
sent from all these formative influences. He was there in the
very beginning. His story was told, and not as though he were
an obscure figure who lived years ago, about whom we have
only hand-me-down knowledge. His presence was experi-

enced. His name was as comfortable in home and church conversations as speaking of a friend who is expected and always welcome. Like any close, personal friend, he is to be appreciated and dealt with, not gossiped about.

Jesus Christ came to be closely bound up with feelings about myself in relation to others, and with challenges to act in certain ways. His name gives firmness even yet to a sense of belonging, of knowing who I am because another calls me by name.

My response has never been neatly packaged. I have to admit there are torn places in the wrapping and dangling pieces of string: feelings of belonging and not belonging, of knowing and not knowing, of doing and not doing.

Nor can I detail the steps by which these elemental feelings and challenges became so intertwined with the story of Jesus. I often wonder about the specific contribution of: singing "Jesus Loves Me" in church and school classes; drawing maps of Palestine in vacation Bible schools; memorizing Scripture passages—earning blue and red cards toward a Bible; taking part in church pageants and various fellowship occasions where people obviously enjoyed being together; trying to beat my pastor in pingpong and rarely doing it; singing in the choir with an attractive girl, later to become my wife; sharing Sunday dinners with family and friends from church and community; hearing parents, preachers, and church school teachers speak of Jesus in the same breath they assured me that our heavenly Father knows the number of hairs on my head, will never give a stone if asked for bread, and cares for me even as he does for birds of the air and lilies of the field.

I am called by name. There's no doubt about it, even though my reply is often unsure. And that calling is mediated by, but reaches beyond relationships in family, church, school, neighborhood. Jesus Christ supports a belief and a prayer, a confidence and a hope: I am free to become the person I was intended to be, *just because* I am called by One who never forgets my name, who knows me with all the caring and reliability of the One who sent him.

A sense of belonging is comforting, almost as essential as breath itself. But the Christ I experience in time and memory is not only associated with being known by name. There's abrasiveness and intrusiveness as well. He calls forth, and gives direction to a sense of being claimed from beyond myself. His call to obedience forces me to remember in spite of my forgetfulness that I'm to love God without ceasing and my neighbor as myself, to turn the other cheek, to go the second mile, to find my life by losing it, to live without anxiety about food, shelter, clothing, financial security, all material possessions—I almost said necessities, but that's the whole point.

Jesus Christ has always presented me with an uncompromising claim to radical obedience. I was formed in a church tradition which has simply assumed that Christ's example is to be followed. His teachings are to be obeyed. If he says we are to wash one another's feet, it's to be done. (It is still common practice in the Church of the Brethren to wash feet, in preparation for a fellowship meal and the bread and cup, during Love Feasts or communion services.) If he says peacemaking is a mark of discipleship, participation in war is to be refused. If he says not to be anxious about worldly things, keep life simple.

I am not saying my church tradition has necessarily been more faithful to this radical claim than any other. Christ's example has not really been followed by me or others around me. His teachings are difficult to obey.

Nor was it easy for me to distinguish between the unqualified claim of Christ and the lesser claims of persons—sincerely motivated—who had strong opinions about who I was and what I should do. "Jesus wouldn't do that." Or was it parents who didn't want me to do it, or preachers, or neighbors, or all together? That's as difficult to pull apart as yeast is from dough once the bread has begun to rise.

I was propelled into baptism at age eleven by a visiting evangelist who convinced me it was time to join church. He made any alternative seem most unattractive. In my tradition baptism is reserved for those who are old enough to decide for themselves, supposedly after reaching the "age of accountability." No one has ever defined that very precisely. I guess I had reached it. The minister immersed me three times, face forward, the way such things are done in the Church of the Brethren.

For all its open-endedness, the decision which I made as an eleven-year-old set a direction for my life. But it was another five years or more before church began to capture basic interests and commitments. I found myself increasingly estranged from church between age eleven and sixteen, years marked by restless searching. I became a high school dropout just as I was about to turn thirteen—remember I began school at five. It was still legal to stop school after eighth grade, and other classmates from our rural Mennonite-Brethren community were stopping. I helped take farm products to market, working at least twelve hours a day, six days a week. I can't imagine why I chose that rather than high school.

I spent what spare time I had hanging around with youth of my own age. We really constituted what now would be called a street gang, only we were congregated in a rural village rather than in a modern city, and we drove cars rather than roam the streets on foot. Our primary adventures were drinking cokes and eating hamburgers by the ton, talking about the girls we rarely managed to date, fast driving, and an occasional trip to such forbidden places as roller-skating rinks or movie establishments in nearby villages. My restlessness grew. My baptismal vows seemed distant, and unrelated to what appeared more pressing at the moment.

Where was Christ in all this? He was there. I didn't think much about it then, but I knew his claim stood head and shoulders above that of family, work, church even gang. Only he deserved my total commitment *just because* he found his life by losing it, having been faithful even to death on the cross and raised victorious.

The call to obedience issued by Jesus Christ is equally an invitation to start over again. His name validates the promise that tomorrow need not be a dreary rerun of yesterday. Because he lives in time and memory, a sense of new beginnings does battle with any sense of being fated. My past is not one inevitability after another controlling present action, but a platform for facing alternatives in openness to a future that is filled with what another purposes for my life.

I didn't have language to express it the same way at age sixteen, but things that were going on then helped to identify Christ with the promise of new beginnings. It happened suddenly. A friend and I were doing some of that fast driving I told you about. The curve was sharp. Like many country roads in the area there was loose gravel along the edge. He lost control of the car. We turned end over end. I remember sparks flying and the smell of hot rubber before we landed upside down in the ditch. There were no seat belts in the car, but somehow we both crawled out uninjured, only badly shaken up.

It would be more dramatic, but less accurate, to say I walked away from the accident a changed person. It was hardly a Damascus road conversion. I don't even recall any split-second review of my life while skidding toward what might have been death.

There had to be more to life than marketing farm products and hanging around with the gang. Of that I was certain. I had been out of school for over three years. By now I knew it was a mistake.

I began to spend more time with the church youth group than the gas station gang. Why not? There I shared in a very active youth program. There I met attractive girls, one named Ruth, instead of only talking about them. Besides, we had a pastor and wife serving our congregation whose life-style I admired greatly.

The claim of Christ was experienced at a new level of intensity, and with maturing readiness to respond. Persons whose judgment I valued said they saw ministerial gifts in me. I was encouraged to pick up my education with a view to church service. Shortly after reaching seventeen I took up residence in a Bible school in New York City, one my pastor and wife had attended. I was enrolled as a special student, and given employment, while taking full-time evening high school classes.

World War II intervened after about a year and a half. I was drafted. Church teachings about nonparticipation in war led me to request noncombatant service. It was granted. I was assigned to the 50th Field Hospital, United States Army, European theater of operations, from 1943 to 46, working most of that time as master sergeant in charge of personnel affairs. I was discharged in January 1946. By September of that year I had studied enough books borrowed from the local high school, and taken enough examinations through the Pennsylvania Department of Public Instruction to earn a high school equivalency diploma. Ruth, who was to become my wife in 1947, earned a diploma the same way. Then came college, ordination to the ministry, seminary and graduate school, with service in the parish, and a vocation as college and seminary teacher and administrator since 1954.

Christ's claim to radical obedience is at the same time an invitation to new beginnings. The promise of newness which his name validates draws upon the contribution of all those persons who are essential to one's formation, but has the backing of God's own forgiveness and power of renewal.

A sense of fundamental rightness bears the name of Jesus Christ. *Just because* he is God's plumb line, he doesn't let me pretend that things are better than they are. He validates the promise that things can be right somehow in spite of what's wrong in me and around me.

That's quite a promise. It is almost as difficult to believe as the promise to Abraham that he would have descendants as plentiful as the sands along the ocean even though Isaac was to be sacrificed, seemingly the last chance for an heir.

There are times when nothing seems right anymore, like those mornings when, still half asleep, a feeling of apprehension sweeps over you. Something about the day is foreboding. When you are fully awake, and you identify what's ahead that's disturbing—facing a crucial decision, asking the boss for a raise, coping with prospects of serious illness, starting a new job, taking an important examination, traveling for business or profession—generalized anxiety may abate somewhat. But you reach for a foundational rightness that is firm, especially when you are disturbed, uncertain, alone, and more than a little afraid.

As a child I remember sitting with parents during Church of the Brethren Love Feasts. The adults washed one another's feet while singing the hymns they knew by heart. I was too young to be a full communicant. The visiting evangelist who precipitated my baptism was still several years away. I did share the fellowship meal of freshly baked, sugar-topped buns, cheese, and hot, creamed, sweetened coffee. Following the meal, and the appropriate scripture readings and prayers, there was the communion bread and cup. I was delighted when the elders slipped me a tiny piece of that unleavened bread, baked by the deacon's wives with precisely the right number of fork imprints on each of the long, narrow strips.

I felt the solemnity of it all. Persons important to me were doing what was important to them. I knew there was no magical erasing of troubles that still bothered parents, friends, and the larger society around us. And yet there it was, just waiting to be experienced and celebrated: the promise of a fundamental rightness whose name is Jesus Christ, a rightness that gathers persons within a circle of care, makes possible new beginnings, and calls for radical faithfulness.

The promise of a rightness that endures, and nothing seems right anymore—these two elemental feelings stand against each other in mortal combat. When total loss of rightness threatens to overwhelm, it's downright scary. We reach toward the promise with the anguish of persons about to slip into quicksand.

Our son, David, was beginning second grade, He had recently learned to write—really to print. When there was a household quarrel about such things as picking up toys, he often stalked into his bedroom and posted his feelings on notes stuck on the door which he usually closed with a slam.

On this particular day he chose instead to send us an air mail letter, a piece of paper folded so that it glided through the hall into the living room where his parents sat. With his permission I'm including a copy of that letter without editing.

Talk about a mixture of feelings doing battle with one another. Things aren't right. We want them to be right again. Disturbed, uncertain, alone, more than a little afraid, David was reaching for relationships—for the promise of a rightness that endures.

Jesus Christ is the very name of God, the signature validating all his promises.

Why do I believe that? Just because![3]

I'm not talking to you
Becuse YOU are rude.!!!!
You helped some so why
not give in see a hand with
picking up?
I feel like running away
But I LOVE You so I will
not.
I'm sorry I yelled at you!
And about the card game
you, do not have to play
it!
I hope you still love
me.
I forgive you. xx. air mail

Just because Christ knows my name with the caring and
reliability of the heavenly Father who sent him.

Just because Christ's unqualified claim on my life is confirmed by his own radical obedience.

Just because Christ's call to faithfulness is also a call to
new beginnings, an invitation to start over again.

Just because Christ's own oneness with the righteousness
of God assures me that things are right somehow, even when
disturbed, uncertain, alone, a little afraid, and more than a
little distressed by the wrong within and around me.

Why . . . ? Just because! That's just the way it is, that's
why.

5

"You ought to be ashamed!"

FREEDOM isn't easily defined. One book after another is written about it, and with good reason, for it's a basic human and Christian theme. Even more than a theme, it's a promised possibility. It's a life-sign that is essential to our personal well-being and to our mutual sharing. It's a health-giving spontaneity almost as necessary as the air we breathe. Words to describe it are important but, like love and trust, freedom is known in the actual experiencing of it. Still, there's nothing private or unspeakable about the down-to-earth relationships within which the freedom we come to know is always waiting to be born.

With the aid of the following word pictures, I shall sketch partly fictional but nonetheless very real situations where freedom emerges—both the freedom *to be* and *to do*.

• Freedom is a teenager deciding not to wear a sweater just because his mother is cold, or perhaps it's wearing the sweater even though it is his mother who is cold.[1]

• Freedom is fighting sleep when your wife/husband wants to talk, or perhaps it's falling asleep and trusting the partner to understand.

• Freedom is refusing to say "I told you so" even though the circumstances confirmed you were right, or perhaps it's saying it with warmth and a twinkle in the eye.

• Freedom is welcoming a family of a different race next door even though the whole neighborhood has been trying to keep them out, saying property values will decline. It's also the courage it takes for a new family to move into an area already so blighted by prejudice.

• Freedom is feeling left out, being noticed, and having someone enlarge the circle to let you in. It's also the sensitivity of the one who notices you are being excluded and does something about it.

• Freedom is being appreciated for who you are, not simply for what you have done. It's also appreciating others on the same terms.

• Freedom is a young adult in a supportive group dealing openly with previously unacknowledged anger toward his upbringing, especially toward parents and church, and coming to accept that past with forgiveness and growing insight. It's also the ability of others, strengthened by his struggle and courage, to relate more openly to their own past.

• Freedom is a voice within each of us that cries out for respect, for creative expression, for the realization of one's deepest potentialities. It's also the anger which erupts if that cry is unheard. The anger may have no other outlet than violence and disorder if that personal center is unjustly threatened and oppressed.

• Freedom is the breath of fresh air that greets prisoners on their release from captivity. The prisons that wall us in are places, but they are also timidity, suspicion, prejudice, stereotyping, inferior educational opportunities, job discrimination, and systematic exclusion of certain ethnic, sexual, and racial groupings form the full benefits of society. The spontaneities that deliver us from bondage include a warm hand clasp, a smile, a word of welcome, a friendly glance, and an open circle of caring persons. Also included are persons risking prison for witnessing to their disturbed conscience about our nation's involvement in aggressive acts in distant places, a task force on securing housing for low income families, legislation to end segregation and to guarantee equal employment opportunities, and the repentance that lets "justice roll down like waters, and righteousness as an ever-flowing stream."

• Freedom is a father playing ball with his teenage son on a Sunday afternoon even though he has just been strongly urged to do so. The urging was accompanied by a forceful reminder that a neighboring father was already playing ball with his son. What turned out to be freeing for the father in this instance was remembering how important it was to have his father play with him when he was his son's age, and letting that reconciling, mediating memory motivate him more than the impulse to assert himself over against the call to action, the obligation or sense of "ought" he has just experienced.

It really is odd the way "ought" sets up an opposition within us, and occasionally gets linked to "shame" in our household encounters. Equally odd are the responses we offer. I can testify to that.

It was a damp, drizzly night in January. Our son, David, had invited two school friends, Dennis and Jim, to play some games in our recreation room. Dennis, who lived next door, went home first because of an early morning paper route. Jim stayed until close to midnight. It was Friday. With no school the next day the lateness presented no problem.

My wife, Ruth, was in the study. I was at the other end of the house in the family room watching television. I overheard Jim indicate it was time for him to leave. Then David offered him a ride. The drizzle had slowed down but it was still somewhat nasty outside. I echoed the invitation from the comfort of my settee just as the late movie was about to reach an exciting conclusion. Jim stated his preference for walking, really jogging, because he likes to keep in shape. That's how he had arrived three hours before. He was quickly out the door and on his way home.

Ruth came quickly into the family room when she realized Jim had gone, having surmised that he was walking but without hearing the offers David and I had made to take him home. She said in a deeply concerned tone of voice: "It's late. Why didn't you give him a ride? I wouldn't want David to walk at this hour of the night. Suppose something happens to him. Wouldn't it have been better to have given him a ride?"

In the Groff household we strive to avoid accusatory ways of expressing feelings and concerns. So "You ought to be ashamed!" is not a frequently used way of speaking to one another. But in this instance both Ruth and I knew that issues of "ought" and "being ashamed" were being raised in profound ways.[2]

I already had some uneasiness about the way it had worked out. I hadn't offered to take Jim home as forcefully as I might. I really wasn't that eager to leave my comfortable settee, get the car out, and miss the end of the movie. I guess I was already feeling more than a little ashamed, even before Ruth questioned me with such genuine concern for Jim's welfare. At any rate, I worked hard to justify my inaction: "Both David and I offered Jim a ride. He's old enough to state his real preference. He's used to jogging. It's not really that late. He can take care of himself. He'll be all right. Let's not be overprotective."

"You ought to be ashamed!" What is the shape of our freedom situations where such an expression intrudes itself? One thing is clear. It has to spring into life from the midst of that complex interplay between shame and ought. Let's pause to think about each of these words, and the life issues they pose for us.

Shame is a complex state of affairs. It's physical. The stomach gets tight. Blood rushes to the head. We blush. Sometimes blushing is almost pleasant, like getting redfaced when we are suddenly made self-conscious about our relation to someone we like very much. But the blushing shame produces is unpleasant. It accompanies the feeling of being caught, of being found out. The action, or compromising situation, doesn't match the picture of the person we like to think—and have others to think—we are. Shame is devastating. We are exposed. We want to run and hide.

Shame is a stranger to none of us. And the shame we experience collects related feelings of awkwardness, embarrassment, regret, chagrin, and guilt, like a dust mop collects dust. Before, and especially after Ruth's intervention in our family room, I regretted my lack of aggressiveness in offering to take David's friend home. If only I had it to do over again. The distance is short enough I could have taken him, and have returned to the conclusion of the movie with greater enjoyment. As it was, I spent far more time and energy working through the resultant feelings and strained family relationships than the trip would have taken. Besides, I did feel guilty, for something might have happened to Jim.

Ought is a small word, but powerful. When someone feels we ought to be or do anything, we realize just how motivating the word is. It may be part of an unreasonable obligation, laid on with a heavy hand. Just as often, though, it is a legitimate expression of concern, an authentic prompting and invitation to be responsible. My wife certainly has been helpful, more than once, in reminding me of what it means to be a good father, to be a good neighbor.

Let's return again to the episode with David's friend. It will be useful to focus the issue of freedom still more sharply in terms of that situation. The Scriptures provide insight. If we place the New Testament and this household encounter side by side some complementary accents are heard.

My failure to take Jim home is clear evidence of apathy on my part (Matthew and James). I surely knew what my obligation was. The choice was clear. The only question was whether I would obey the requirement, or the law, of good neighborliness.

The episode reveals how vulnerable I was to deception (John). I not only failed to make an appropriate response, but allowed myself to live in illusion, to make excuses, to rationalize my inaction. I consented to the thought that a legitimate requirement of good neighborliness is actually unreasonable. After all, Jim was old enough to know his own mind. Anyway, he likes jogging, and it's no doubt good for him.

The situation disclosed my behind-the-scenes questioning of whether I am my brother's keeper (Paul). The interchange between Ruth and me looms especially large when viewed through Pauline lenses. Ruth's admonishments evoked a heightened sense of obligation. Whenever that happens the temptation is to challenge the authority of the one doing the admonishing. Whether overt or not, we are prone to ask: "Who are you to say what I shall be and do?"

These new Testament accents have one thing in common. They presuppose the Old Testament story of Adam and Eve. Recall the garden setting, so admirably suited to the needs of those earliest inhabitants (Gen. 1–3). Adam and Eve could move freely in their paradise. But there was one irritation, one limit on their ability to do just what they pleased. God said they could not eat of the fruit of the tree planted in the center of the garden.

We know the outcome of the story. Adam and Eve disobeyed. They ate the fruit. God sought them out. He didn't come saying: "You ought to be ashamed!" He didn't need to. They were already in hiding. Even the hastily gathered fig leaves couldn't conceal their blushing. Shame had overtaken them.

Matthew and James are most attuned to the note of disobedience in the story. God's command was reasonable and clear. Adam and Eve faced a choice between the way of life and the way of death. They chose the latter and had to suffer the consequences.

John is concerned about the role of the serpent in the downfall of Adam and Eve. He is sensitive to the way we are all victimized by illusion, by mistaking falsehood for truth, by failing to see even though the light of God's truth is as bright as the sun.

Paul identifies the problem of Adam and Eve, indeed of all their descendants, as one of authority. Hence, it is the tree in the center of the garden that becomes the chief stumbling block. It precipitates a prideful, subversive questioning. Who says we ought to be or do anything? If we are to be free, can we tolerate any limiting authority over against us? Must we be accountable to someone else? The asking presupposes we are in hiding, already covering ourselves with makeshift fig aprons. Not the eating of the forbidden fruit, but the questioning of whether we are accountable—that's where it all starts.

This questioning stands prior to all our relationships. It snakes its way into everything we do. It coils around our memories and anticipations, making us protective and anxious. It lurks in the grass waiting to strike. A call to mutuality and discipline has been planted in the heart of life itself. Freedom is experienced only where there is accountability. But the questioning is always there—from the very beginning.

It's the very fact of an ought, a limit, a tree that leads to the questioning I've been talking about. Some oughts deserve ready compliance while others do not. But we are as ready to challenge its authority when the ought is an authentic prompting as when it's a heavy-handed imposition. God's own tree in our midst fares no better than any other. That's the subtlety and shame of it all. We experience freedom only as it rises somehow from the depth of this very earthiness, this bondage, this shame.

With the force of new life springing out of death, freedom is called forth from the mixed-up state of personal-social affairs in which we all live. We are grateful for everything that helps deliver us from those indignities which dehumanize. And yet the shame of our human condition is that we seek security in the wrong places. We stubbornly cling to attitudes of racial or group superiority. We are self-protective in our relationships with others, based on fear and threat. We desire to hold on to personal and institutional privileges. We go-it-alone rather than risk the vulnerability of that open interchange which always marks true community.

All of us participate in, and are affected by, society's institutions that have been designed to meet basic political, economic, family leisure, educational, health, and religious needs. Institutions are intricate and ponderous. They contribute to human welfare, but also add their own subtleties to the way freedom and unfreedom intermingle.

These corporate arrangements are vulnerable to that subversive questioning and shame which all began when Adam and Eve were driven from the garden. Who says I must be accountable? Am I my brother's keeper? Such challenges to the authority of the tree which God placed in the center of things have gone underground to form a labyrinth of rationalizations, depersonalized assumptions, perceptions, and routinized ways of doing things.

Established patterns for distributing goods and services favor some races and discriminate against others. Racism infects social systems with their many interconnected parts, and not just the attitudes of individuals. Inequities also accrue to minority status, sex, age, religion, or social class. It's hard to pinpoint responsibility and to know where to take hold when grasping for creative solutions. It's difficult to bring about needed changes in structures as well as in attitudes.

Persons and groups are still being discriminated against in such areas as housing, job opportunities, and education. This goes on in spite of equal rights legislation and humani-

tarian appeals. Difficulty in coping with institutional rigidities
is no excuse for hand-wringing apathy on anyone's part. Refusal to face the complexities is scarcely helpful either. Sim-
plistic, slogan-ridden appeals in support of one cause or
another will not be adequate to deal with the many social ills.
Our problems require careful research. But there is need for
courage and faithfulness at the level of active deed.

The church as institution is also troubled by its rigidities,
its defensive hedgings against new relationships and ways of
working, its preoccupations with group identity and social approval, its pride in charitable deeds. Still, healing spontaneities keep surfacing, bringing deliverance in the very midst of
our shame. A life-giving power is at work, doing battle
against those false securities which offer only bondage and
death.

It is helpful to recall what the apostle Paul says about law
against the background of the struggle to be accountable, the
questioning and the shame, whose beginnings are as ancient
as Adam and Eve (Rom. 7–8). Connotations of the law in
Paul's many references to it include the Ten Commandments,
and the detailed rules that grew up around them, as these
rules were promoted by religious groups like the Pharisees in
their concern to ensure meticulous obedience. He is inti-
mately acquainted with the interior conflict that results when
the law intrudes itself in human affairs.

With shocking candor Paul says he would not have known
sin apart from the law. Slyly working its way through the
commandment, "You shall not covet," is the seductive power
of sin, stimulating "all kinds of covetousness . . . the very
commandment which promised life proved to be death for me.
For sin, finding opportunity in the commandment, deceived
me and by it killed me.

Does this mean that the law is sin? "By no means! It was
sin, working death in me through what is good, in order that
sin might be shown to be sin, and through the commandment
might become sin beyond measure."

Paul is caught in underground warfare between false securities and healing spontaneities. Here the protagonists in the
battle are death and life, bondage and freedom, life in the
flesh and life in the Spirit. "For I delight in the law of God, in

my inmost self, but I see in my members another law at war with the law of my mind and making me captive to the law of sin which dwells in my members. Wretched man that I am! Who will deliver me from this body of death?"

He finds it difficult to do those things he knows he ought to do even though he wishes to do them. "I do not understand my own actions. For I do not do what I want, but I do the very thing I hate."

Because of the deceptions that constitute the "body of death" from which we need deliverance, the law commands but cannot motivate. It points the way toward freedom but doesn't take us very far in that direction. It demands selflessness but fosters self-centered preoccupations and pride. It plants an authoritative claim in the center of life that is potentially liberating but that constantly triggers rebellious opposition. There is no freedom apart from obedience to the commandments that are essential disciplines in the life promised to us by God, but we keep stumbling over ourselves and each other in our efforts to be accountable. We can't resist the temptation to ask: "By whose authority does anyone say I ought to be or do anything?"

What is needed is a mediator who intervenes, who steps into our death, bondage, and shame, who successfully combats the seductive powers of sin. Such a mediator transforms the law of harsh command into the law of love, and frees us to welcome it as a trusted friend rather than to resist it as an alien intruder. Such a mediator frees us from the captivity of our false securities, from our authority hang-ups, and frees us for the "love of God and neighbor."

Paul has such a mediator in mind when he writes: "For the law of the Spirit of life in Christ Jesus has set me free from the law of sin and death. For God has done what the law, weakened by the flesh, could not do: sending his own Son in the likeness of sinful flesh and for sin, he condemned sin in the flesh, in order that the just requirement of the law might be fulfilled in us, who walk not according to the flesh but according to the Spirit. . . . To set the mind on the flesh is death, but to set the mind on the Spirit is life and peace."

The law continues to intrude an authoritative ought or tree into the center of things. It calls us to accountability before God and neighbor. But that call has now been set within a renewed relationship based on the loving trustworthiness of a man sent from God whose own testing in Gethsemane, the garden spoiled by human rebellion, issued in obedience and death on the cross. Because of his mediation, his going ahead to run interference, the law formerly linked with sin and death now offers life and peace to those whose minds are set on the law of the Spirit.

The sin we need deliverance from cuts beneath individual actions in violation of moral standards. It's the whole mixed-up state of human affairs, personal and corporate, which has been infiltrated by self-protectiveness, prejudice, and anxiety-prone withdrawal from the risk and promise of relationships. It's not the shame we all experience, except as our shame signals the prideful questioning that precedes our hiding, the futile efforts to cover our nakedness with fig leaves, and the excuses which only deepen our captivity.

The power of healing, or grace, that breaks into our confused situation does more than offer a choice between two alternatives, between life in the flesh and life in the spirit. We are the recipients of the love, faith, and trust of One who has done battle at the level of the underground warfare between our false securities and the freeing spontaneities. Skirmishes continue in that conflict, but the outcome is no longer in doubt. Victory is foreshadowed in Christ's own life and obedience which proved to be stronger than death itself.

What we are confronted with, through Paul's version of the Christian story, is an invitation to surrender to a relationship already established, a relationship marked by love and fidelity. Love demands that we commit ourselves without full knowledge of what may come of it, a type of dying to one's self-protectiveness with faith and hope that new life will be received in return. This is one way to understand what Paul has in mind when he speaks of sharing Christ's death and resurrection.

To set one's mind on life in the Spirit is to accept the requirement of love that we decide for it ahead of those absolute guarantees which life in the flesh would dictate. This has always been the direction of God's authoritative claim placed in the center of things. As we look out from our hiding places,

to obey God's claim may seem risky indeed. But along with
Abraham, Isaac, Jacob, and their numerous descendants, indeed with the whole of humanity, we are asked to respond to
that startling law of love with its rigor and promise of freedom, its promise of personal fulfillment through mutual accountability.

In these ways Paul has contributed substantially to our
reflections about the struggle for freedom. His reading of the
human situation carries forward one recurrent form of the
Christian story, as this story in turn is rooted in the Jewish
scriptures. But we have seen that Paul's rendition is not the
only one. Even as the New Testament gives us three ways of
accenting the Adam and Eve story, and the episode with
David's friend, so there are three supplementary versions of
the "good news," of Christ's role in delivering us from bondage, in granting us the gift of freedom.

Matthew and James are concerned about the danger of
apathy, about disobedience, about the loss of down-to-earth
practicality in matters of faith. Christ is the One who sets
forth the disciplines of God's present kingdom. His teachings
and example are clear. They are to be followed without tor-
tured laments about "not being able to do what one wants to
do." Obedient discipleship is an ever-present possibility if we
but choose to heed Christ's commands, and draw strength
from his living Spirit within the community of believers.

John worries about our strange inability to grasp the
truth, our inexplicable stumbling around in the dark. We allow ourselves to be deceived into thinking that the "objects"
of our fears and suspicions are real, when in fact they are not.
And so we keep giving them a type of pseudo-reality with
destructive potential. But Christ is the light that overcomes
the powers of darkness, of superstition and stubborn blind-
ness. He offers his own life and way as the "truth that sets us
free." We may live in that truth if we but open our eyes and
see.

Paul understands the central issue to be pride and our
defiant rejection of accountability. Even the law, a definite
part of God's good plan of creation, gets caught in our questioning and shame, and triggers a person-destroying opposition. The only answer is a power of grace, of healing,

sufficient to attack the problem in its depth. What is needed is a mediator, a reconciler, one who "stands between" and thus liberates us from bondage. Jesus Christ is that mediator. He is the healing memory that frees a father to play ball with his son even though he has just been reminded that he ought to do so.

Christ sets us free. He does not come saying: "You ought to be ashamed!" He already finds us in hiding. But he calls us forth from our prison walls. He doesn't simply point the way. He is the way. All we have to do is face toward him and walk, eyes on him and not on the floor, confident that whenever we die to self and rise to the "love of God and neighbor" we share his freedom. For that quality of love means never having to say, "I am ashamed!"

6

"It's all your fault!"

IF I WERE ever to compile a collection of life's embarrassing moments," this incident would surely be included. I was driving the first car my wife and I ever owned, having bought it less than a year before. We were at a busy intersection in New Haven, Connecticut, seeking to turn left. The 1939 Plymouth had no automatic turn signals. So the window was down, and my arm was outstretched to indicate my intention.

The flow of cars was heavy in all directions. There was no traffic light. A policeman was standing on the curb, watching but not actually directing things. I did not realize until minutes later that he expected left-turners, at the slightest opportunity, to intrude themselves directly in front of oncoming drivers who, once a driver had signaled and entered the turn, were expected to yield the right of way.

Since there was almost no break in the line of cars coming toward me, and I felt somewhat cautious, especially with the policeman gazing at me, I sat there, arm ramrodded out the window, car poised for action at my command. I'm not sure how long I would have remained there, except for the jarring words of the policeman: "Turn! What are you waiting for? Better watch your arm. It might drop off!" Somehow we made it through the intersection safely and were on our way.

Over thirty years later I not only recall the incident but also how I felt: embarrassed, awkward, self-conscious, frustrated, ashamed, angry, self-righteous. Surely I was more right in being cautious than the policeman thought I was. For some time thereafter my wife listened to my outbursts: "What did he want of me?" "I always thought policemen expected drivers to be cautious, not reckless." "Why was he just standing on the curb, rather than directing traffic where he belonged?" "I don't see how I was in the wrong; surely he's more to blame than I."

Even now I am a bit shamefaced about the incident. No amount of rationalization has eliminated the feeling of being painfully vulnerable, of being exposed. Good drivers are neither reckless nor excessively timid. In seeking to avoid one extreme I edged toward the other. The policeman's shout struck me as unnecessarily rude, but it had power because he was in touch with a boundary limit, a criterion of safe driving, which I accept as true and binding.

The episode did not call forth the indignation I felt on other occasions when I wanted to kick against the very fact of a limit or authoritative standard which holds me accountable. Rather, the temptation was to fall into self-deception. For a time at least, I allowed myself to be convinced that my cautious approach was completely reasonable. Related to this was the temptation to indulge in excuses, in efforts to get myself off the hook by projecting the blame on others, or on external circumstances: "The drivers in the oncoming cars were coming so fast! Why didn't they slow down?" "There should be a traffic light at such a busy intersection." "Why wasn't the policeman directing traffic?" "It's really all his fault!"

In life's embarrassing moments we not only become uncomfortable, but we voice our discomfort in various ways. We sense that others are looking at us. We feel their gaze and, like a small child, we wish to turn our head, even run and hide. Sharp words pierce our defenses and add to the embarrassment, to the shame we are already experiencing: "Watch your arm. It might drop off!"

To deepen our thoughts about moments like my encounter with the policeman, let's again return to the story of Adam and Eve. In the last chapter I outlined different New Testament accents, those of Matthew and James, of John, and of Paul. Paul's insights on freedom and our struggle to be accountable were on the center stage. That meant we were especially attentive to the tree in the garden, or God's authoritative claim in our midst, and the human tendency to challenge it: "By what right does anyone, even God, tell me what I ought to be or do?" We noted that shame is a symptom rather than the cause, or even the direct result of that prideful, self-assertive questioning.

In this chapter we shall stand closer to John and his typical accents. We shall deal, as a result, less with the problem of authority and more with the issue of deception. We shall look more closely at the role of the serpent in the downfall of Adam and Eve.

God's creative work culminated in the calling forth of human creatures, male and female, so marvelously suited to one another, fashioned in the image of their Creator (Gen. 3:1-24). But the serpent was also there, just waiting to inveigle himself with the subtlety for which he is noted. The serpent posed his first question to Eve with deliberate exaggeration: "Did God say, 'You shall not eat of any tree of the garden'?" Obviously God had not. Eve set the record straight. It was only the tree which was "in the midst of the garden" that was out of bounds.

But the seed of doubt had been sown, and well watered; so it quickly sprang into life. Soon Eve had become convinced that her fascination with the forbidden tree was perfectly reasonable, since the tree was able to satisfy two legitimate desires, for food and beauty. It was all so plain to see. Why should God declare the tree off limits? Was he trying to protect his own prerogatives? Eve took of the forbidden fruit and ate. She gave some to her husband, and he ate. "Then the eyes of both were opened; and they knew that they were naked; and they sewed fig leaves together and made themselves aprons."

The storyteller wastes few words as the account continues. God called to Adam: "Where are you?" Adam said: "I was afraid, because I was naked; and I hid myself." God said, "Who told you that you were naked? Have you eaten of the tree of which I commanded you not to eat?" The purpose of this questioning was not to give God information he lacked. Rather, it was to lead Adam and Eve to the place where they would recognize and admit what they had done. As the questioning continued, one excuse quickly followed another. Adam said, "It was the woman you created to be with me who gave me fruit of the tree, and I ate." Then God said to Eve, "What have you done?" Eve said, "The serpent deceived me, and I ate." So the blame was tossed around like a hot potato, first toward God, then toward the woman, and finally toward the serpent. The price of the deception was high: expulsion from the garden.

Adam and Eve are well-established in the thoughts and feelings of all persons who have in any way been touched by the Judeo-Christian tradition. They are central characters in what has become a story-shaping story. This story was itself inspired by, even as it gave dramatic expression to, some of Israel's deepest experiences and convictions. Although presented in the freehand style of a lively tale rather than in systematic, thematic form, these foundational beliefs are implied in, or at least clustered around, the account of the first man and woman: (1) God's purpose is the plumb line that marks off reality from illusion, truth from falsity, straightforwardness from deceit; (2) God is as faithful in judgment as in sticking to his original intention in creation, and in keeping the covenant promises which he made even in the face of human rebellion; (3) God's purpose is not set aside by the serpent's capacity to convince Adam and Eve and their descendants that to believe a lie is more secure, more reasonable, than to follow that way of life and truth which is marked by obedience to God's command.

God's truthfulness and ingenuity in accomplishing his purpose provide the secure context and the infallible standard for measuring the human response. That's what enabled the biblical writers to see that the deception which gripped Adam and Eve repeats itself, with expulsion from the garden as its inevitable consequence. They discerned a common pattern in the experience of Israel, indeed in the human story writ large. Promising beginnings are marred by seduction and betrayal, followed by personal suffering and the disintegration of community life.[1]

Saul's kingly reign began at one of the many junctures between God's purpose (reality) and what seemed more reasonable to the people (illusion). See 1 Samuel 10–13. God intended that Israel should be directly ruled by him in a continuing theocracy. His intermediaries were anointed judges, or Spirit-filled leaders. The people desired a king so they might be as other nations. Samuel tried his best to dissuade them, but the people persisted. Finally, God granted the request, counseling Samuel that he should not take the matter as a personal affront. But, as always, God's initiative had to be reckoned with. Even before the general election got under way, with the casting of lots at a place called Mizpah, Samuel had been instructed to consecrate Saul, not to lead the people in the way of the nations but in the way of God's anointed.

The terms of Saul's anointing charted the direction of his expected obedience, and also set the stage for his temptation. Humility and fidelity in covenant rather than the external trappings of sovereignty and national glory were the "kingly" marks God intended for his "servant." But Saul allowed himself to be diverted from the path of reality by the urgings of the people who, like the serpent, voiced the seductive lie which led to Saul's downfall.

Two episodes in 1 Samuel help describe how all this came about. In the one (1 Sam. 13:1–14), Saul and the Israelite army faced the threat of the Philistines who had mustered "thirty thousand chariots, and six thousand horsemen, and troops like the sand on the seashore in multitude." Saul waited seven days for Samuel to arrive at Gilgal to perform the necessary sacrifices before battle. That was the agreed-upon time. But Samuel did not arrive. The people were scattering out of fear. Morale among the fighting men was at an all-time low. Something had to be done, and soon. So Saul offered the burnt offering. In so doing he stepped over the boundary limits of his office, and infringed upon the appointed duties of Samuel.

The deed had scarcely been done before Samuel appeared on the scene. With a show of outward courage that barely camouflaged his inward trembling, Saul went out to meet him and tried to greet him as if all were normal. But Samuel went directly to the heart of the matter by asking, "What have you done?" Samuel was not seeking information. Rather, he was penetrating Saul's transparent facade, and inviting a confession. Saul explained that Samuel's lateness caused him to take things in his own hands. The people obviously needed his strong initiative. But Samuel was unrelenting. He said to Saul, "Your action was foolish. Now your kingdom has been forfeited because you have not obeyed God's command."

If I put myself in Saul's place, especially in light of my own encounter with the policeman I told you about earlier, I am sure that excuses would have been tumbling over each other: "Why was Samuel so slow in arriving?" "After all, something had to be done, for the Philistines were jeopardizing our 'national security'." "Besides, the people couldn't tolerate the uncertainty any longer. I really did it for them!"

But the Scriptures never let us kid ourselves for long. To obey God's command is the "way of truth and life." That alone is the reasonable path no matter how unreasonable walking in it may be made to appear through the serpentine questioning that always lurks close at hand. Disobedience is the "way of deceit and death."

In the second episode (1 Sam. 15:1–35), Saul engaged the Amalekites in battle. The command was to "go and smite Amalek, and utterly destroy all that they have; do not spare them, but kill both man and woman, infant and suckling, ox and sheep." At this time many still thought that it was an act of dutiful sacrifice to the god of battle to offer up every piece of booty. That whole view of sacrifice, formerly thought to be pleasing to the God of Israel, was eventually repudiated.

The point of this incident cuts deeper than the highly debatable practice which set the stage for Saul's temptation. In the Promised Land no less than in Paradise, persons are surrounded by possible distractions, ambiguities, open-ended situations, choices, and the God who seems unreasonable, or at least obscure. Yet God's gift of life carries with it the command to obey.

But Saul allowed the people to sway him. It seemed so reasonable, even humane, to disobey. So "Saul and the people spared Agag, and the best of the sheep and of the oxen and of the fatlings, and the lambs, and all that was good." Notice, they kept the best for themselves and delivered up only what was left over.

Again Saul sought to hide, to cover himself with fig leaves, when confronted by Samuel. At first he tried to bluff his way through, saying, "I have performed the commandment of the Lord." But even while Saul was loudly protesting his innocence, the sound of bleating sheep and bellowing oxen made it difficult for his words to be heard. Then Saul tried to shift the blame on the people. "They did it! They took of the spoil."

In a last-ditch effort to exonerate himself and his accomplices, he suggested that the booty was spared for a subsequent sacrifice to God. This occasioned one of the most striking prophetic assertions to be found in the scriptures. Samuel said: "Has the Lord as great delight in burnt offerings and sacrifices, as in obeying the voice of the Lord? Behold, to obey is better than sacrifice, and to hearken than the fat of rams."

The Scriptures cover a long span of time and experience. As we have seen, there are different accents or points of view in the various books. But the line of interpretation we have been following is by no means marginal. Well before the rise of the monarchy in Israel, Aaron excused the "golden calf" affair (Ex. 32:1-35) on the grounds that during Moses' long absence on Mount Sinai the people persuaded him to make an object of worship that was more visible, more manageable, more predictable and comfortable. After all, they did not know what had become of Moses or the God he claimed to represent. They needed the security that comes from a deity that is directly accessible without the aura of mystery they found so irritating. But their disobedience brought death. Apart from Moses' intercession, God's wrath threatened totally to consume Aaron and the "stiff-necked people." Judgment came, but so did the mercy which Moses had sought. A remnant was spared.

Life has to be lived outside the garden because of the recurrent deception which subverts us all. This is a strong note which is sounded often in the Scriptures. In fact, it is one way to orchestrate the biblical story as a whole, and, by inference, the story of the total human family. What began with such promise at the time of Israel's exodus from Egypt, and the dramatic escape through the Red Sea, was quickly marred by defections which issued in protracted wanderings in the wilderness.

The new beginnings associated with crossing the Jordan, and the arrival in Palestine, were also quickly overshadowed by temptation and faithlessness. The baalim, or nature deities linked with farming and fertility of the land, seemed more available to the people than the God whom a series of appointed spokesmen from Joshua to Samuel sought to have them obey. There was great subtlety in the enticement of the baalim. During the years in the wilderness the Israelites had been roving nomads. When they reached the Promised Land it was indeed flowing with milk and honey, a veritable paradise compared to the desert from which they had come. The local inhabitants had obviously mastered the secrets of tilling the soil, and devoutly sought the aid of their deities. Why shouldn't the Israelites be equally prudent and solicitous, since they too desired rich harvests? It was all so reasonable. Why should the God of Abraham, Isaac, and Jacob be so jealous?

We have already seen that the monarchy which began at the clamoring of the people fell into disarray. It wasn't only Saul who was taken in by the lie that somehow seemed more believable than the truth of God's command. David was no less tempted to forget that he was the anointed servant of God's purpose and at times assumed the prerogatives of an absolute monarch. To satisfy his lust for Bathsheba, David had her husband, Uriah, sent to the place of most intense fighting in a battle where he would surely be killed.

Ahab's violence against a commoner came about because he was seduced by Jezebel and her greed for Naboth's luxurious vineyard. An epitaph suited to many of Israel's kings during this period would be: "He feared the people and obeyed their voice." The disastrous consequences are well-documented in the Scriptures. The nation of Israel underwent one captivity after another, to say nothing of inner division and strife.

This larger story of Israel provides the backdrop for the life and ministry of Jesus. It would have been easy for him to stand with Saul and all others who have chosen the way of the nations rather than the way of God's anointed. Even his closest disciples voiced the lie in suggesting that he should abort his mission which seemed to be leading to inevitable suffering and death (Mark 8:31-33). How would God's purpose ever be achieved if he gave up his life? How then could he be instrumental in the coming of that kingdom of peace and justice they all awaited? These thoughts must have appeared very reasonable to Jesus. It obviously required great dedication and insight for him to spot the deception, and to reject it: "Get behind me, Satan! For you are not on the side of God, but of men."

Jesus' temptation came in different forms, all subtle and highly believable. Why not replace the rigors of obedient servanthood with a ministry marked by spectacular miracles? Why not take up the sword with its predictable powers? Or why not adopt a policy of playing it safe, of accommodating to those in control? Jesus' obedience in the wilderness (Matt. 4:1-11) and in his own garden of testing (Mark 14:32-42) makes a bold contrast to the disobedience which figures so prominently in all other responses.

The "triumphal entry" into Jerusalem illustrates the way Jesus' ministry was persistently misinterpreted by the crowds (Mark 11:1-10). Jesus rode on a donkey, a beast of burden. Prophetic tradition saw this as a symbol of humility, of service, of peace. Yet as he rode the crowds ran alongside him shouting, "Hosanna to the Son of David." Jesus came on a donkey, symbolizing his status as God's anointed. The crowds greeted him with palm branches, signifying royalty and military power. Jesus was walking in the way of obedience even unto death on the cross. The crowds walked with him because they hoped he might lead them in the way of the nations.

Jesus not only came preaching and walking in the way God intended for his creation; he is the very embodiment of that intention. He is "the way, the truth, and the life." His repudiation of the seductive lie and his submission to the will of the Father constitute the only sure path to the restoration of

life in the garden, or to the kingdom lifestyle marked by justice, love, and humility before God.

The Scriptures face the perplexing problem of continuing
seduction and disobedience in the human story even though
Christ lived and died for us all. How does one account for that
ongoing rebellion? Is it human stubbornness (Matthew and
James)? Is it the failure of the law which sets up a death-
dealing conflict between "ought" and "wish," where the
mere fact that something is commanded gets in the way of our
obedience (Paul)? Is it a vulnerability to deception that somehow manages to darken the skies in spite of the bright sunlight
of God's truth and reality in Jesus Christ (John)?

The biblical story repeatedly grapples with the mystery of
that seductive lie which is rooted in the very center of an
otherwise good creation. This mystery eventually issued in
the thought that we not only have to reckon with the "lie" but
with the "liar." It cried out for an adequate symbol. The particular shape of that symbol emerged only gradually, and with
continuing modifications along the way. The Adam and Eve
story emphasized the deception as such, and lodged its source
very generally in one of the creatures, in the serpent. By the
time of John's Gospel, however, we find explicit reference to
the devil who is said to be the "father of lies" (John 8:44).

In view of many dehumanizing events that deeply disturb
us—Hiroshima, Buchenwald, Vietnam, Watergate—we sense
that persons and groups do indeed act as though they were
possessed, or at least victimized. Likely we do not find the
symbol of the devil as convincing as earlier generations. But I
believe we are in danger of removing the devil too easily from
our contemporary consciousness. Dostoevsky once said, "If
God goes, humanity goes." I should like to come at the same
insight from its reverse side and say, "If the devil goes, compassion goes." In wrestling with the devil, and the subversive
tendencies he symbolizes, we face into an ongoing personal
and corporate struggle of tremendous proportions. If that
struggle is not open and sharply focused, humanity itself is
threatened.

I am not advocating particular ways of imagining the
devil, such as with horns, long tail, and cloven hoofs. The
issue is not whether we picture him as a person. Nor do I

commend any kind of belief statement like, "I believe in the devil." In fact, there would be something extremely odd about such a claim. It could never be on the same level as the affirmation, "I believe in God."

What is really at stake? Nothing less than the ability to cope with our vulnerability to deception, with its cumulative character and destructive potential. At its best the Judeo-Christian story features hardheaded realism in assessing the human situation and yet supports compassion, both God's compassion toward us and our own toward one another and ourselves.

Think of God's lament for his people who, as Hosea pictures them, steadfastly insist on playing the harlot: "How can I give you up, O Ephraim! How can I hand you over, O Israel! . . . My heart recoils within me, my compassion grows warm and tender" (Hos. 11:8).

Or, to take one more example, recall Jesus' anguish: "O Jerusalem, Jerusalem, killing the prophets and stoning those who are sent to you! How often would I have gathered your children together as a hen gathers her brood under her wings, and you would not" (Matt. 23:37). The Scriptures invite us to believe that at the heart of the universe we meet not only firmness but also concern, not only justice but love, not only righteousness but compassion.

The Scriptures are clear that we face life and death choices. God is biased in favor of the poor, the outcasts, those who are held captive. He is always the advocate of "justice that rolls down like waters, and righteousness that flows as a mighty stream" (Amos 5:24). He is steadfast in covenant and expects similar fidelity from us. Therefore, the issue is not whether we are to take sides, but on which side we stand. "I have set before you life and death, blessing and curse; therefore choose life" (Deut. 30:19). "Seek good, and not evil, that you may live" (Amos 5:14). "Hate what is evil, hold fast to what is good" (Amos 5:15).

We are required to cope with the subtlety and power of the devil. He intrudes the lie even in the midst of what might potentially be our most promising moments and deeds. But the compassion our vulnerability arouses in the biblical story never compromises the challenge to decisiveness. There is no encouragement whatever for the fence-sitting, wishy-washiness of uninvolved persons.

There is strong support for joy on the part of all who elect what God stands for. The devil has not won. God's partisanship on behalf of his creation reaches even to the point of his suffering love. The culmination of that refusal to abandon his wayward creation is the life, death, and resurrection of Jesus Christ. Through this person who is the way of life and truth victory is assured over sin, law, death, and the devil. Crucial battles are yet to be fought against the alien "principalities and powers" which somehow manage to hang on, but the outcome of the war has been established. God's purpose is not overcome by those hostile forces which strive to subvert it.

If the devil goes, compassion goes. That's a dramatic way of making the point that the Scriptures have the capacity to hold things together which otherwise get fragmented. Compassion qualifies but in no way dulls the call to accountability. In sinning we allow ourselves to be deceived, no matter how clever is the enemy against which we struggle. We are held responsible because the goodness of God's creation is reinforced by his own action even at tremendous cost to himself. A life of joy and confidence becomes possible because God's love has the quality of a father who is willing to see his own son suffer and die that others might live.

This "good news" shapes our thoughts and deeds. To the extent it becomes the inner "story of our lives" we experience the freedom which the scriptures celebrate and promise.

Freedom is needed from too much indulgent, self-protectiveness. The racist attitudes and rigidities of a white, middle-class suburbanite are one illustration of what I have in mind. Such a person assumes that things are the way they are for good reason, and little should be done to disturb the status quo. Members of other races, such as blacks, need more patience. It takes time for social change to come about. Besides, look at all the advances that have been made. Blacks can ride buses and eat in restaurants with far less restrictions. They are securing more and better jobs. Educational levels are rising. Why aren't they content? The organized agitation which has often accompanied the civil rights movement is deplorable.

Law and order must be preserved at all costs. Violence is to be punished.

The deception in all this becomes clear when measured by the biblical story. Members of a given society's establishment, which includes all those who have a disproportionate amount of that society's advantages, are always tempted to accept their benefits as evidence of virtue and hard labor. Privilege tends to arouse protective instincts. If we happen to be among the favored ones, we have much to gain from social stability even though the economic and political system violates many who, through no fault of their own, are among the disadvantaged.

Freedom is required not only from such false perceptions and the self-protectiveness they foster, but also from too much hatred or generalized anger. A black militant from a Chicago ghetto addressed an assembly of white suburbanites. He insisted that we were directly responsible for the sins of earlier generations that led to the enslavement and impoverishment of blacks in America. With clenched fists and hard eyes he told us that no white persons in the room really had any right to live. If he were in our shoes, the only appropriate response he could imagine would be suicide.

The overt "clenched fists" and "hard eyes" of the black militant, in some ways, are more justifiable in light of the biblical story than the covert actions and feelings of those from the advantaged segments of society. His humanity has been violated by entrenched injustice. His hatred, and shotgun blasts of anger, witness to his God-given right to be treated as a person, with full dignity and fair access to society's rewards, rather than discriminated against by racist institutions and persons.

I am not placing the two examples on exactly the same footing, or implying that our problems would be solved if both parties became more moderate. A level of institutional personal repentance is required of the white suburbanite that would be less reasonable to expect of the black militant. And yet compassion is essential to the advantaged and the disadvantaged. On that level of human need there is common ground. Only those attitudes and actions which spring out of compassion are unqualifiedly freeing. They alone signal that liberation whose name is Jesus Christ. The only way off the tiresome treadmill of protectiveness and hostility, of attack and counterattack, is that compassion whose foundation is God's own suffering love.

This series of short sayings will summarize my main points:

Charitable deeds without compassion equals paternalism, a posture often and rightly attacked nowadays by those who feel its sting.

Acceptance of one another without compassion equals apathy, for then we scarcely have acceptance at all, only toleration.

Confrontation without compassion equals angry rebuttals, which means that the whole encounter has been neither prophetic nor reconciling "according to the Scriptures."

In the long run, we may all be better off if the devil goes, but not if compassion goes with him. For then, indeed, the devil will turn out to be the winner after all.[2]

7

"Be good!
Stay out of trouble!"

As an eight-year-old I could get pretty impatient when things didn't go my way. I had just rushed through my Saturday morning chores and still had not received permission from my parents to play with my best friend. I knew it would take at least twenty minutes to get to his house even if I hurried. He lived over a mile away, near Lederach, Pennsylvania.

The path I needed to take meandered lazily across an uncultivated, overgrown field. The field was part of an abandoned farm located near our home. I was always fascinated and a little afraid as the old barn with its crumbling walls came into view, and as I saw the empty house with its broken-out windows gaping at me. My speed would quicken as I passed the barn and house. I could also save time by cutting across the exposed concrete and stones that were part of the dam in the creek which separated me from my destination. This creek is known as the Branch, because it's a tributary of the larger Perkiomen River. I could take still another shortcut through Camp Wa Wa, which would be idle now that the Philadelphia youth who came here each summer were back in school.

Even so, I was eager to be out the door and on my way. My parents were not pleased with this pastime, but my friend and I planned to play with our toy guns. These we made out of carefully selected lengths of wood which served as the gun barrels. We used nails as the triggers and clothespins as handles which were held in place by a strip of tire tube drawn taut, and which could release another piece of tube that had been stretched to its outer limit. There was enough force in our projectiles to sting whenever we were hit during our frenzied skirmishes.

Tiring of that, we would knot an empty burlap bag into a tightly rolled ball and play tag by attempting to hit one another with it. We would climb to the highest sections of the barn's rafters and jump into the hay that smelled of clover and catnip. We would catch frogs in the farm pond. Or we would sprawl on the living room floor to match wits in a lengthy game of Monopoly.

Finally my persistence prevailed. I was given permission to leave. The parting admonition was one I often heard from my parents: "Be good! Stay out of trouble!"

Neither my parents nor I had to pause long to sense what was implied in that familiar household expression. I was not to pry into things that were none of my business, or to intrude myself into places where I did not belong. I was to be careful in handling toys and dishes so as to avoid breaking or spilling. I was not to let my youthful exuberance run away with me. My tendency to "play hard" was to be held in check so that neither I nor others around me would get hurt.

The admonition also signaled concern for my safety. It was a wish that I might not get my feet wet, or suffer a more calamitous fate while crossing the dam. Permission to make the journey was based on the knowledge that I had done so before, and that the water held no serious danger for me since I had already learned to swim quite well. I regularly fished and trapped all along the creek on my own. Had my parents known of my climbing to dizzying heights in the barn as part of our play activity, their consent might have been harder to come by. Of course, they knew that harm could befall me without any clear connection between my misfortunes and my misdeeds. So at the deepest level, the exhortation to "stay out of trouble" was a prayer, a benediction, that might have been stated this way: "Let no trouble come to you, whether that trouble is of your own making or not."

Then too, this benediction implied the hope that I would dutifully embody family ideals. I was to be courteous and obedient to my elders. My whole deportment was to reflect gratitude for the hospitality extended to me, and I was to say "Thank you!" for particular favors received. I was to be tidy, always remembering to wipe my feet before entering my friend's house. I was not to be a troublemaker unless I needed to intervene on behalf of a younger playmate who sometimes joined us, even though that intervention would surely get me in trouble with my friend who loved to gang up on anyone smaller. I somewhat enjoyed doing the same thing, so on this point and others I didn't always live up to expected standards. At any rate, I left the house keenly aware that I was to be the "good" son of whom my parents could be proud.

Neither life nor the Scriptures presents us with trouble neatly sorted into the types that I am about to sketch. By definition it would not be trouble unless experienced in very untidy ways and situations. Still, some important distinctions have begun to disclose themselves through this initial reading of experiential data, and a little arranging of them will help keep our discussion focussed as we proceed.

Trouble is the price tag attached to the rough-and-ready manner in which we develop as persons. It signals human inquisitiveness and creative drives that keep breaking established routines. It follows from the inner need to grow and to learn new things. At any age we learn by venturing; by trusting the environment to support our probes; by touching and occasionally knocking over and disarranging; by assuming that a goal can be reached even though others are sure it cannot; by pulling items apart to see what makes them go, and perhaps failing to get them back together again; by wanting to try things for ourselves although those more experienced could do them better and faster.

After spending time with their grandchildren, doting grandparents often say about them: "They're certainly live wires!" That usually means delight in their healthy sprightliness, and relief at not having to carry full responsibility for their growing up. Grandparents have lived long enough to be

acutely aware of both the enjoyment and the exasperation involved in human development. Since they no longer have the
active role they had in raising their own children, they are
freer to celebrate the deep satisfaction parents also feel in
spite of the trouble which predictably is coming along the
way.

Trouble is a steady companion because no meaningful
relationship between persons—parent and child, husband and
wife, friend and friend, neighbor and neighbor—comes pre-
fabricated. Each relationship demands ingenuity and recipro-
cal learning. Each must be entered into as a brand-
new-venture, no matter how much practical wisdom may
gather around the socialization process. Getting along with
one another is a lifetime project, and we all know firsthand
the many struggles that project entails.

Trouble results from our misdeeds. We get the trouble that
we deserve. Shamefacedly we confess our responsibility for
our difficulties. "I was so preoccupied that I was halfway
through the intersection before I saw the red light. I'm so
grateful that traffic wasn't heavy or it might have been worse.
A policeman happened to be there. He gave me a ticket, but I
have only myself to blame."

*Trouble involves misfortunes for which no clear explana-
tion can be given.* We get more trouble than we deserve.
From the loneliness and pain of serious illness the cry is
heard: "Why me? What have I done to be singled out like
this?" In those moments we feel overwhelmed by the trouble
that seems so inexplicable. We long for persons who, out of
their strength, are willing to stand with us in our weakness.
We lean heavily on such persons, with their gifts of empathy
and care, their tears of compassion. They give us hope that a
brighter tomorrow will yet dawn.

*Trouble follows from the difficulty of living up to those
ideals that lay claim to us.* It comes from dreaming dreams
that run ahead of things as they are. Even though earthbound,
we persistently reach for the stars. There is among us the urge
to radicalize, to "act out" the values which are often only
given lip service in home, church, and society. Active inter-
ventions are made on behalf of those suffering from injustices
that are not of their own making. All of us are strengthened by

active troublemakers who are genuinely attuned to a higher righteousness and who respond not out of mere obstreperousness or rowdiness but out of a disciplined conscience.

Trouble comes in these many different sizes and shapes. The biblical story promises no easy release from the conflicts involved. Being in trouble because of dedication to the "kingdom and its righteousness" is very close to its central story line. Jesus Christ is its title and master image. He not only taught but lived a childlike trust in the trustworthiness of the heavenly Father. There is no evidence that he went looking for trouble. He didn't need to. Given his commitment, trouble went looking for him. The gospels provide very few details about his growing up, but there are some hints that preoccupation with his "Father's business" got him in difficulty with his parents and teachers at a very early age (Luke 2:41–51). During his adult ministry his friends thought he was "beside himself" (Mark 3:21). He was an embarrassment to his mother and brothers (Matt. 12:46–50). He was misunderstood by his closest disciples (Mark 8:31–33). Religious authorities and government officials viewed him as a troublemaker and kept him under constant surveillance. His threat to the establishment became so intense that he eventually was put to death on the cross. He is the clearest example of one who was "persecuted for righteousness sake."[1]

Because of its focus on Jesus Christ, the biblical story challenges assumptions that become commonplace in the household. When I was told, "Be good! Stay out of trouble!" I knew that I was expected to be and to do just that. But Jesus Christ confirms what I began to recognize even then. To be good and to stay out of trouble are not as easily accomplished together as the familiar admonition implies.[2]

Being a parent myself, I have more respect now than as an eight-year-old for tidy, efficient, trouble-free households. I am glad for any child's dutifulness, teachability, respect for elders, and general sense of what constitutes good behavior. I am not critical of my upbringing which featured similar values. During his youth, our son surely felt such imperatives and expectations, which occasionally were liturgized in our benedictions as he left the house to play with a friend. I trust he also caught our prayerful wistfulness on his behalf: "Let no trouble befall you, either through your own misdeeds or those inexplicable misfortunes that threaten us all. If you must get in trouble let it be the price of faithfulness to your truest convictions."

Our son is now an adult. That means I am freer to think and feel like the grandparent I hope to be someday. The active righteousness of God breaks through all differences of sex and age, marital status, and having or not having children. Still, as we have seen, grandparents have a special vocation to help celebrate the deep satisfactions of being parents, which often get obscured by the heaviness of direct parental responsibility for rearing children. Beyond that, grandparents form a natural partnership with children and youth since they all tend to feel that parents, and other adults who make up the large "middle group," have institutional, financial, even physical resources greater than their own. That encourages them to rely heavily on the shared metaphors and ideals to which all have more direct access. Such metaphors and ideals are the powerful motivators in any social grouping, and their force is never lessened, but more often intensified, when voiced by the child or youth who carries a group's future, or by the grandparent who embodies a group's treasured past.

I am no longer a child and only a grandparent by anticipation. But in "that day" I shall see clearly, what I now only see dimly, that tidiness and decorum in the household are less important than a growing child's exuberance, determination to do things for oneself, curiosity about the contents of the kitchen cupboard and every unopened drawer in the house, capacity for spontaneous shouts and laughter, and endless questioning about the whys and wherefores of life. In "that day" I shall delight in those youthful spirits among us— whatever their chronological age—who are convinced that a better job can be done in combatting injustice, and have the courage to follow through on their conviction. In "that day" I shall understand that being good as qualified by a New Testament life-style often means getting in rather than staying out of trouble.

The biblical story accents faithfulness for righteousness' sake. It invites persons of all ages, and in all circumstances of life, to face toward a trust-filled future. When we face toward that future, household preferences for safety and orderliness are turned on their head in the ways just described. We experience freedom in our struggles to relate to one another and to embody our nobler ideals.

The Scriptures also challenge some literary forms as they bear on our misdeeds and difficult-to-explain misfortunes. My examples will be drawn from both the classical and the popular arts.

The Scriptures challenge the *morality play* approach to storytelling in which options are thought to be unambiguous and the consequences proportional to right and wrong acts. Contemporary "westerns," so prevalent on television, evidence the enduring popularity of this dramatic style where the good is easily distinguishable from the bad. Even when the odds seem stacked against persons wearing "white hats," they triumph in the end and thoroughly rout the villains.

The Scriptures reflect the attractiveness of this clear-cut choice system, which is adaptable to many interesting variations in plot and dramatic action. The would-be comforters of Job must have lived by such a system, for they tried their best to convince him that he brought his calamities on himself, perhaps through some nearly forgotten indiscretion in the past. Eliphaz even drew a direct parallel between iniquity and trouble. "Think now, who that was innocent ever perished? Or where were the upright cut off? . . . those who plow iniquity and sow trouble reap the same" (Job 4:7–8). The author of this ancient story makes us feel the appeal of what Eliphaz and his associates kept saying, but he also works hard to show its limitations. Our misdeeds are rooted in pride, deception, and a disobedience that is as ancient as Adam and Eve. They do issue in suffering, expulsion from the garden, and death.

But misfortunes are not strictly proportional to misdeeds. It is not a matter of simple poetic justice where each get only what is deserved. The innocent are hurt (Job 6:21–30). The unscrupulous go unscathed. Suffering and death confront us with a mystery that resists our best efforts to explain it. God is merciful in his might (Job 38:1—2:6). Even in our frailty, in our moments of utter hopelessness when he seems intent on "slaying us," he allows us to defend our "ways to his face" (Job 13:15). That's the basis for a trust that endures, even when all grounds for trust seem to have washed away.

Jesus sided with the author of the book of Job. One day he was asked, "Rabbi, who sinned, this man or his parents, that he was born blind?" Jesus replied, "It was not that this man sinned, or his parents, but that the works of God might be made manifest in him" (John 9:2).

Another literary style that is challenged is a *tragedy,* in which our misfortunes spring from ignorance more than misdirected loyalty and will. Disaster comes inevitably because we are required to act although, in our temporality, we have only a very limited knowledge of things. Even when we refuse to decide, as a way of protesting our distance from eternity, time keeps passing. There is no escaping the inexorable encroachments of fate. We can face our destiny with stoical courage, purged as much as possible of pretensions and emotions that only deepen our plight.

If a morality play presupposes sharp distinctions between good and evil, and clear-cut choices which make a difference, a tragedy blurs them together. To illustrate, let's imagine a fictional case in line with classical Greek tragedy. A young warrior returns to his home area after enforced exile of long duration, falls in love and marries the beautiful woman whose household he had purged of intrusive freeloaders, only to discover that the woman is his sister. What is good from a temporal standpoint turns out to be the very opposite when seen from an eternal perspective which, tragically, is inaccessible to the warrior until it is too late to save him from the disastrous consequences of an incestuous relationship.

I have stripped these forms of storytelling to their barest essentials. They are often presented in highly imaginative ways, and rich with subtle embellishments. By cutting behind those embellishments though, we can easily pinpoint their essential differences from dominant tendencies in the biblical story.

As the ground of righteousness, truth, and love, God marks off clear boundary lines between good and evil. These lines are not blurred by any talk of eternal as contrasted with temporal perspectives. There are highly consequential differences in perception between God and his creatures. His covenant purpose, which carries his life-stirring command at its very center, is made to appear unreasonable. But that apparent unreasonableness stems less from our lack of knowledge (as in a tragedy), and more from wilfully mistaking wherein our true security is to be found. We are not fated to succumb to the lie which inexplicably lurks in the midst of God's good creation, or to the devil as the "father of lies." We are not destined to walk in the way of deceit and death, or to rebel against the authoritative claim that we be accountable to and for one another under God.

We come to personhood nowadays in an environment already infected with prideful, disobedient, illusion-ridden actions of previous generations, and that infection has taken on a health-destroying aggressiveness of its own in opposition to the righteousness and peace God intends for his creation. There is a strong note of compassion in the biblical story, but not as a basis for those excuses which are really symptomatic of the underlying distortion. We are held responsible, and we are expected to join God's own partisan struggles against the evil which still manages to hang on, even though it has no status within God's intention.

None of this fits the scheme of simple poetic justice that we often find in a morality play. Such a scheme can even help prompt the proud, rebellion-filled assertion that the poor who are enslaved in contemporary ghettos are there because that's exactly what they ask for. "If they really wanted to work and better themselves, they could," is only one form of the serpentine reasoning that keeps tempting us. But persons do not always get exactly what they deserve, whether life's ledger happens to show largely credits or debits at a given time. Our misfortunes are surrounded by a shadowy edge of mystery. Somehow, that mystery stands before the misdeed, as the questioning of our accountability is prior to eating the forbidden fruit.

Life has its centeredness and its fulfillment in God's purpose. The Scriptures never waver on this affirmative note. That purpose, and the character of our relation to it, are misunderstood if likened uncritically to a *detective mystery*. In such storytelling the problem of "Who did it?" is thought to be soluble as soon as a shrewd-enough sleuth comes along. It is soluble in the terms already set by the completed events that posed the problem. Once we learn that the culprit was really a wayfarer who just happened along, rather than the butler or the jilted lover, there are no leftover shadowy edges. All the clues then fall into place like the pieces of a jigsaw puzzle. The reader moves from the "beginning" (past) toward the "end" (future), with suspense (present) hanging on the question of how quickly the sleuth, and all armchair assistants, can penetrate the secret of what has already happened.

In sharp contrast, the biblical story, with its accent on God's purpose, is more like an artistic creation that is still coming into being. Think of the way an on-purpose act ties quite separate moments and undertakings into a secure bundle by means of a deeply interior, invisible bond. I set out to write a chapter dealing with "being good" and "staying out of trouble." If the chapter comes off with artistic power, my purpose brings coherence to what is said from the very first word through each successive sentence and paragraph, until we are caught up in a fellowship of shared experience and understanding. The direction is from the end (future) which is incarnate in the beginning (past) and in all subsequent moments of surprise and discovery (present) as mutuality of life and thought emerges.

God is the creative artist whose sensitivity and skill are boundless. His covenant markings of righteousness and peace, of justice and love, foreshadow the end (future) which, from the very beginning (past), shapes life (present) in its direction. The distinctive accent in the biblical story is Jesus Christ, the story's title and controlling image. He is more than an adept sleuth who lets us in on the secret about events that have already happened.

Rather than the clue that closes the case, Jesus is the clue that opens life to the purpose of God. He is the sentence that illuminates and informs every other sentence and paragraph in a story to be told, a story which we are all helping to write. He orients us as much toward what is yet to be as toward what has been. He is the unity of future (Father) and past (Son), as that unity promises to gather every present moment into itself (Spirit).

Because of who he is we draw strength from what he does. Jesus Christ exemplifies the "blessedness" of one who is "persecuted for righteousness' sake." He empowers us to be good in terms of his own convenantal sturdiness, even though it means getting in rather than staying out of trouble.

Beyond that, he weaves the unbreakable thread of sacrificial love into the fabric of the universe. He stands between God's covenant purpose and every alien rigidity that rips and tears at it. The wrath of opposing forces is most intense just where God's victory is most dramatic. Trouble threatens to overwhelm just where God's active righteousness establishes its firmest bridgehead. Purposelessness seems to gain the upperhand just where God renews the promise that his creation is indeed positioned toward that end which, from the beginning, has been holding it all together. For in Jesus Christ, the one "who has borne our griefs and carried our sorrows" (Is. 53:4), we meet the Omega who is also the Alpha, the Lord God, "who is and who was and who is to come, the Almighty" (Rev. 1:8).

8

"Say thank you!"

WE OFTEN hear and say, "Thank you!" and in a variety of circumstances. These words easily become routine. In expressing them we may go through the motions without depth of feeling or thought. Still, we recognize them as an integral part of any suitable response to a personal service or courtesy.

The checker at the local grocery store finishes bagging my purchases and dismisses me with a "Thank you!" I reply, "Thank *you!*" or "You're welcome!"

My wife, Ruth, knows that one of my "favorite things" is potato pie, served hot, with butter and warm milk. I walk in the door on a cloudy, depressing day, to find one baking in the oven and suddenly the "sound of music" fills the air and "then I don't feel so bad." The change of mood is reflected in the tone of my voice: "What a welcome surprise. Thank you!"

Later the assembled family sits down to the meal and prays, "Thank you, God, for the joys of food and family, for all your gifts."

"Thank you!" These words signify the contentment that comes when our daily needs are met. They celebrate our caring and being cared for within innermost family relationships. They express our appreciation for good friends. They fit just as comfortably amidst those broader associations and incidental contracts that filter through our workaday world.

Thanks spring out of thankfulness, or gratitude as a fundamental life orientation. Kind deeds nurture our ability to say, "Thank you!" But gratitude stands prior to, and reaches beyond them all. Gratitude is superior to ingratitude as the underlying tone of attitudes and actions. This we know in the same way we know that caring is better than callousness, that integrity is to be preferred over deceit, and trust over distrust.

Gratitude is a mark of authentic humanity. It is a highly desirable, actually an essential personal quality. Parents sense this when they give such care to the prompting of their children upon receipt of a favor. The litany usually goes like this: "What do you say?" If nothing is forthcoming, the coaching gets more insistent: "Say thank you!"

Involved, no doubt, is the desire to develop social politeness. But parental concern to teach the language for gratitude and the practice of verbalizing it cut deeper than mere custom and the regard for community approval.

Gratitude is an inward spontaneity which signals a maturing person. How terrible the loss if anything preempts that person's ability to receive a favor gratefully, if anything diminishes the thankful acceptance of life itself as a gift, a grace, which far exceeds efforts to earn it.

Gratitude carries within itself the urge to act. There is an impulse to find appropriate symbols: flowers, cards, a handclasp, a song, an embrace. It craves a symbol big enough to do it justice. Given its bias toward fullness of expression, that craving is not satisfied by anything partial. Each "Thank you!" presses for a suitable way of naming the gratitude that gathers up, but extends beyond, particular acts of kindness and even beyond persons who are closest to us.

"Thank you, Ruth, for surprising me with a potato pie, indeed, for all you mean to me." Not to divert attention from, but as a way of celebrating that act and intimate relationship, I join in the household affirmation, "Thank you, God, for the joys of family and food."

A "Thank you!" does not necessarily lead one to its foundations in thankfulness, and then, by direct implication or intuition, to belief in God as the source of all that's good. To say that gratitude yearns for a symbol big enough to do it justice, and confessionally to affirm God as that symbol, is not to present an argument from gratitude to prove his existence. Such reasoning could not be any more convincing than traditional arguments from causality (God as First Cause), contingency (God as the Unconditioned), and adaptiveness in the universe (God as Designer). The God we come to know in Jesus Christ meets us on his terms, and his unqualified claim challenges all lesser commitments. The voluntaryism is also from our side as we respond in faith or unfaith.

Still, each "Thank you!" does point beyond itself. With the same "just because" forcefulness we talked about in an earlier chapter, I believe that pointing is toward this fuller affirmation: "Thank you, God!" (praise). Other elemental needs and aspirations are aimed in the same direction: "Help me, God!" (petition); "Forgive me, God!" (penitence); and "Help him/her, God!" (intercession). These are basic experiences around which prayer and worship cluster. I find my own spiritual life anchored by their roots, with their trimness and ability to hold fast even when change lashes away at them.

Parents sense the importance of admonishing children to say, "Thank you!" I wonder if homes and churches nowadays do as well teaching appropriate habits of praying and worshiping.[1] Knowing suitable words and other symbolic forms does not guarantee depth of spirituality. Any elaborations, even those found in the Lord's prayer, draw their strength from these "inward groanings" with their stark simplicity: "Thank you, God!" "Forgive me, God!" "Help me, God!" "Help him/her, God!" But there is no guarantee either in deliberately sidestepping the question of artistry and adequacy of worship aids. Jesus had harsh rebukes for hyprocritical praying (Matt. 6:5–8), but he also responded to the plea of his disciples: "Lord, teach us to pray" (Luke 11:1–4).

Its foundational role in prayer and worship is related to another characteristic of gratitude. It is a gift freely given and freely to be accepted. As such, it asks for no apologies. It requires no hedging about with safeguards or assurances of its intention and worth. It has no need whatever to prove itself.

Our common ways of speaking are insightful. It would be highly inappropriate to respond to someone's "Thank you!"

with qualifiers: "What do you mean by that?" "Prove it!" Gratitude is to be received at its face value with a simple return of "Thank *you!*" or "You are welcome!"

Given the kind of world we live in, and our cumulative human failures, the gift of gratitude positions us toward inevitable life tensions.

"Thank you, God, for those I love and those who love me." But what about those who are alone? Those isolated from circles of care and intimacy? Those lacking bonds of affection that remain firm and convincing?

"Thank you, God, for daily bread." But what about those who have too little or no bread at all?

"Thank you, God, for work I enjoy." I make little distinction between work and play, I feel a large measure of support from faculty and student colleagues, and receive high job satisfaction—with a few moments of frustration thrown in. But what about those who find little fulfillment in their work? Those who are bogged down in dreary, unchanging routines? Those who work only to live and can hardly wait for weekends? Those who have little chance of being surprised by the unexpected and the new?

The Scriptures steadily position us toward a life of faith that issues in obedient works, toward a life of gratitude that overflows in fitting neighbor-oriented responses. Paul accents justification by grace. So the movement is from faith to works. Our freedom in Christ is not to be used as "an opportunity for the flesh," but through love we are to "be servants of one another" (Gal. 5:13). "For in Christ Jesus neither circumcision nor uncircumcision is of any avail, but faith working through love" (Gal. 5:6). "For the whole law is fulfilled in one word, 'You shall love your neighbor as yourself'" (Gal. 5:14).

James accents works, with faith as the indispensable presupposition. "Religion that is pure and undefiled before God and the Father is this: to visit orphans and widows in their affliction, and to keep oneself unstained from the world" (Jas. 1:27). "Faith by itself, if it has no works, is dead" (Jas. 2:17).

James believes that obedient discipleship is more possible than what Paul implies in his laments about doing what we don't want to do, and not doing what we intend (Rom. 7:19). The claim of Christ presses in upon us every moment with an invitation and the power to respond. That is a helpful reminder. However, unless we listen equally well to Paul we may forget that our holiness, our righteousness, is not grounded in ourselves, but in the freedom of Christ's Spirit. We may carry a heavy load of guilt about our failings. We may find it difficult to accept the gift of gratitude. Out of sincere yearnings for evidence of growth in Christlikeness, we may even challenge one another to obedience in a tone of voice that sounds like we are shoring up someone's "Thank you!" with qualifiers: "What do you mean by that? Prove it!"

All of us are challenged by the tensions gratitude thrusts upon us.[2] We face the inevitable interplay between justifying faith and obedient works. No carefully worded statement can guarantee true integration between gratitude and neighbor-oriented responses. Only Christ and his Spirit can do that. But I am led to this affirmation: Gratitude develops the feet and hands of loving service, not because it is shored up in any way by us or challenged to do so, not because it is required to prove itself, but simply because it is gratitude.

Gratitude places us within a power of grace that is liberating. That grace bears the name of Jesus Christ. Through the righteousness and peace that became flesh in him, we are enabled to be and to do what otherwise remains impossible. His obedience holds together what our disobedience pulls apart. He is the bridge over that "ugly, wide ditch" which yawns between a complacency that can never weep, and a glum moodiness that can never smile; between the inability to sing and be glad, and the inability to lament on behalf of those who have so much less to be glad about; between the delusion that we can't do anything and don't try, and the presumption that we can do everything if we but try hard enough.

In Jesus Christ we are free to accept the gift of gratitude, to accept it joyously, to praise God from whom all blessings flow. In him we have the right to be grateful without guilt, to receive the gift of life and all its blessings with a "Thank you, God!" on our hearts and lips.

In Jesus Christ we are constrained to weep over the distance between the ideal and the actual, to grieve that people are hungry, cold and ill-housed, to cry out with voice and deed against the injustices that tear at our common humanity.

The liberation that gratitude supports works itself out in deeds of loving service, not because we heroically decide that it shall be so, but simply because it is the freedom Christ gives. We stand in the faith, the obedience, the gratitude of the One who lived, ministered, died, and lives at the right hand of the Father that we might all say, "Thank you!" and mean it.

9

"Tell me a story!"

TELL ME a story!" That urgent appeal is heard in every household where children are free to make their wishes known. The delight of children in stories is as inevitable as the falls and minor hurts of their growing up. Enthusiasm runs high whether the story is read or recited, whether it is a legacy from the past created "out of nothing" by the story-teller, whether it is new or has been heard many times before.

When it comes to stories we are all children at heart. Whatever our age, we find something deeply satisfying about a tale well told. A "time to come" (the end toward which the story points) anticipates itself in a "once upon a time" (the story's beginning) and gathers us into the "story time" along the way. If we find ourselves captured by the story, with its suspenseful conflicts and hoped-for resolutions, then story time *(kairos)* transforms our clock time *(chronos)*. Story time is measured more by significance and intensity of involvement than by seconds ticking away. We all love story time for it binds future, past and present into a purpose-filled unity. Through the integrating power of a story our experience is less fragmentary, less lonely, less a matter of one unrelated occurrence after another. We are participants in a larger whole.

From its earliest beginnings the church has depended upon the story it tells in order to be itself. That story is based on the Scriptures which, in turn, have the form of episodes within episodes, of actions and anticipations, of happenings and meanings, reaching toward a story line, a title, which holds it all together. The story's title is Jesus Christ in whom all persons and events, indeed all history and creation have their focus. The story line is God's purpose which points us toward the "fulness of time" when all things shall be gathered as one "in Christ." That promised time is in unity with the foundations of the world, and in unity with every other time, including our own. "For he has made known to us in all wisdom and insight the mystery of his will, according to his purpose which he set forth in Christ as a plan for the fulness of time, to unite all things in him, things in heaven and things on earth" (Eph. 1:9–10).

To become a believer is to obey the story's story line. It is to belong to the servant people under the servanthood of Christ. It is voluntarily to accept our place within the story of God's purpose, the story the church tells as a way of experiencing its own identity, the story we tell as the "story of our lives."

We tell the story that has already been told. We do not reconstruct it from scratch in every generation. We share a cumulative memory, both oral and written, with primary foundations in the Scriptures.[1] Prior to your version or mine the story of God's purpose stands as a living heritage of faith. It is an objective check on private whim and fancy.

We tell the story as a means of personal appropriation. The story remains distant, even incomplete, until our telling is added. It invites our paraphrase, in word no less than in life. Let me offer such a paraphrase in the hope that I shall stimulate you to make your own. You will quickly catch the central images of storytelling and God as Storyteller in my rendition:

Before it all began there was the Storyteller
* before anyone ever said, "Once upon a time"*
*   before characters, plot, and story line*
*   before galaxies, Milky Way, and any planet's birth*
*   before sun and moon and spaceship earth.*

The Storyteller loved stories, so
  persons were created
    to hear them
      to tell them
        to live them
          to create them.

Persons were created in the Storyteller's image
  reflecting the same artistic skill
    not as puppets on a string
      but as living beings with memory, heart, and will.

The Storyteller sketched the story line
  tend the garden
    live for one another, not yourself alone
      pursue your neighbor's good
        as though it were your own
          help create a story of covenant and care
            where peace prevails because the people share
              where the rights and privileges of all are cherished
              where equity and fairness are fed and nourished.

Storytelling is fraught with danger and terror
  once given breath of their own
    characters become obstreperous
      and fall deeply into error
        my neighbor seems so threatening
          more like an obstacle over which to climb
            how can our destinies be so closely intertwined
              who says I am subject to another's command
              isn't life safer when ruled by my own hand.

That lie is so believable
  so graceful and smooth
    even the Storyteller's truth
      by comparison
        seems awkward and uncouth.

That lie is two-faced as Dr. Jekyl and Mr. Hyde
   appearing as a smiling, seductive rival
      to the Storyteller's command
         then fading into a fearsome
            flaming apparition
               that divides us
                  from the Promised Land.

That lie rips and tears its way all through the story
   an unintended holocaust
      without sanction in the Storyteller's script
         leaving death and heartbreak in its wake
            gathering force as persons keep falling victim
               to the lie's mistake.

The Storyteller stands steadfast in face of all resisting
   whose story line points toward the end
      that is also our true beginning
         whose judgment and mercy are equally persisting
            opposing all pride, rebellion, and deception
               while groaning with the whole creation
                  which yearns for its redemption.

In the fullness of time a child appeared
   the light of truth shone in his face
      born from deep within the storyteller's mind and heart
      born of woman in a given time and place.

Behold the man
   the people said he came to destroy the old
      he said he came to make all things new
         he dreamed a dream of human community
            where justice and love eliminate all strife
               where persons love their enemies
                  make peace their aim
                     turn the other cheek
                        go the second mile
                           and trust the trustworthiness of life.

Behold the man
  in him the end
    which pulls at us from the beginning
    has its midpoint on the way
      Storyteller and story line become a single action
      a unity of what's promised and the person
        whose light of truth charts the overall direction.

Behold the man
  they nailed him to a tree
    convinced he was a threat
      but just when its power seemed most powerful
      the death-dealing lie more than met its match
        humility was not overcome by pride
          obedience stood firm against rebellion
          and trust was not seduced or set aside.

Behold the man
  an example who empowers
    one who stands between us and the enemy
    a victor over life-destroying error
      he is all that and more
        through his oneness with the Storyteller's purpose
        even death is driven out the door
        in our dying he too knows death
        in his victory
          even though we die
          we too shall live.

The Storyteller's story is yet to be completed
  each new creation invites another level of completion
  each character must walk the way of truth
  or wander aimlessly amid confusion
    as person and institution look ahead by looking back
    and live the life of one we nailed upon the tree
      then all creation is filled with promise
      its claim to confidence as certain
        as the truth that sets us free.

The storyteller's story moves to "another level of comple-tion" when it shapes our life-style. Apart from specific evi-dences of that shaping influence our telling of the story has a hollow sound. It is a clanging symbol and sounding brass. But that caution must not be stressed at the expense of an equally important insight. We tell the story not only *because* we live it but *in order to* live it. Indeed, to tell it as *our* story is to live it.

The focus of the story is not upon our virtues, our hero-ism, or our discipleship. Its focus is upon God's purpose and the outworkings of that purpose as the story unfolds. Its focus is upon the Storyteller, whose intentions and initiatives shape our own.

Our deepest symbolic gestures, storytelling included, are not simply reflective of what is the case. A symbol is not "merely a symbol." Granted, symbols are not magical in their power. But they are also not accidental or secondary to what is going on. They are primary to the activity itself. They are effective means of positioning ourselves with tiptoe expect-ancy toward the coming into being of underlying feelings and tendencies to act. We embrace one another *because* we care, and *in order to* care. We shed a tear in face of someone's bereavement *because* we have compassion, and *in order to* be compassionate. We observe various ordinances (or sacraments)—baptism, Love Feast and Communion, anointing—*because* we are obedient and *in order* to be obedi-ent to Christ's command. Similarly, we tell the story *because* we live it and *in order* to live it.

A problem connected with the church's storytelling is the way the story seems to become increasingly secondhanded as it is passed on from one person to another. Later generations struggle to recapture the fervor and primary experiences of an earlier time.

Elie Wiesel helps us grasp this struggle by telling a story. When Rabbi Baal Shem-Tov saw misfortune threatening the Jews, he would go into the forest, light a fire, say a prayer; and the misfortune would be averted. Time moved on. At long last, when Rabbi Israel of Rizhyn had to face misfortune on behalf of the people, he said: "I am unable to light the fire and I do not know the prayer; I cannot even find the place in the forest. All I can do is to tell the story and this must be sufficient." And it was.[2]

There is power in telling the story even when we cannot light the fire, say the prayer, or find the place in the forest. But that very telling stimulates a restless searching for something closer to original passions and experiences. Persons and groups are sure to come along who ask: "Who says we can only tell the story?" They wish equal access to lighting the fire, saying the prayer, and finding the place.[3]

Any story as ancient as the one the church tells about God's purpose sets up the tendency to dwell on earlier times when the zeal of the story's followers must have been greater than our own. We like to think of our predecessors as more devout and disciplined than we are today. Measuring the present by the standard of an idealized picture of more fervent beginnings becomes an important means of the story's renewal. But sober analysis indicates that earlier times also reflected uncertainties and varying levels of commitment. The story is distant not simply in terms of clock time but of personal significance or story time. Whether in the 1980s or—A.D. 33, the story remains secondhanded until voluntarily appropriated as the story of one's life, until it becomes the story we tell in order to be ourselves.

Another difficulty is overidentification of the story with vested interests and privileges. The fault lies not with the story but with the living and telling of it. Because of the accidents of race, sex, and birth in a developed country, some persons and groups have access to a disproportionate share of the world's goods. It is tempting to perpetuate attitudes and structures designed to maintain those advantages. The way of control and domination seems safer than the way of the servant. Thus, the story becomes tangled in a sticky web of protectiveness. And storytelling itself becomes deceiving since the storytellers are deceived, or victimized by the lie which "rips and tears its way all through the story. . . ."[4]

Particular accents and paraphrases become part of a group's self-understanding. Discipleship, servanthood, peace making, voluntaryism in belief, simple life, community—such themes keep commending themselves to me in my paraphrasing of the story. They spring from my roots in the Church of the Brethren, and the broader Free Church tradition. We all gain an essential sense of identity through a great variety of cohesive fellowships and movements, including the denomination to which we belong. One's particular heritage of faith understandably predisposes one toward certain accents and clusters of teachings. It is fitting that these be held with conviction and nondefensiveness. None of us would advocate an "anything goes" attitude in important matters of belief and practice.

But protectiveness also wraps its tentacles around the subgroupings and traditions which nurture us. A we-they dichotomy all too easily develops. Almost without realizing it we universalize the metaphors and meanings of the story that have laid special claim to us. Others who do not belong to our in-group become "they," and "they" should believe just as "we" do. We-they divisions within the church are at least as old as the Apostle Paul's agonies with the Corinthians. "For it has been reported to me by Chloe's people that there is quarreling among you, my brethren. What I mean is that each one of you says, 'I belong to Paul,' or 'I belong to Apollos,' or 'I belong to Cephas,' or 'I belong to Christ.' Is Christ divided?" (1 Cor. 1:11–13a).

I am confident that the story can outwit our partial renditions and our misinterpretations. The story is not fragile. It is more like the second, third, or even fourth baby in a family. It can stand our rough and tumble treatment of it. It transcends our deceptions and our provincialisms. Every "Babylonian captivity" to which we subject it is turned with realistic hopefulness toward the "return of the exiles."

The story's durability, inclusiveness, and self-correcting powers do not work against firmness in what we believe. They do not require that we play down the insights that are shaped by particular group histories. But the story constantly intrudes this question as an unwavering plumbline in our midst: "Is Christ divided?"

Still another problem is the story's silence. A growing number of persons nowadays are "unable to believe that human life is rendered ultimately meaningful by being incorporated into a story."[5] Such persons not only cannot light the fire, or say the prayer, or find the place in the forest, but they cannot even tell the story.

The story of God's purpose seems subdued in comparison to the cacophony associated with all its rivals. We do well to listen to the silences as well as the sounds of the story. This book was been written in the belief that the story is still capable of being heard, even when the only sound seems to be the silence itself. The story's impact often comes with startling unexpectedness and transformation of the whole context out of which we live, with ongoing reorientation of what we think and do.

Have you ever walked into a house to which you have easy access and wondered if anybody was there? Perhaps it's where a close friend or relative lives. It may be your own home. I occasionally go in our door and begin talking, assuming my wife and son are nearby, only to be greeted by silence. Rather quickly that silence draws a response from me such as: "Anybody home?" I may even take a quick tour of the house before realizing that my wife is working in the garden and my son is next door with a friend.

Expectation and surprise intermingle in such a situation. I arrive expecting to find my wife and son at home. I start talking only to be surprised by the silence. I am equally surprised and glad when I discover that they have been nearby all the time.

"Anybody home?" These words, by analogy, pointed beyond the household. They signal our yearning for a caring presence in the universe, for Someone capable of responding to our deepest hungers and aspirations. Our desire for personal relationships, our achievements and celebrations, our conflicts with persons who mean the most to us, our whimpering about the difficulty of trying to think of others while thinking of ourselves, our preoccupation with safety, our passion to help our children grow, our hope that things can be held together even when everything seems to be pulling apart, our stirrings of gladness, our defiance, our bold declarations, our wistfulness, all are hurled outward. It's as though we were asking: "Anybody home?"

By faith, by walking in the way of Christ's servanthood, we are caught up in the story time of God's purpose. Then we sense that someone is at home. The God from whom Jesus came, the God Jesus taught us to call our heavenly Father, has been nearby all the time.

Then, even as we hurl our concerns toward the silence, surprise mingles with our expectation and our uncertainty. Obedient discipleship brings with it the capacity to hear the joyous sounds of his presence.

Then we have a story to live. We have a story to tell. It's a story with a promise and a name at the center of it. God has kept every promise he ever made, and Jesus Christ is the signature guaranteeing that it shall be so.

It's the "old, old story of Jesus and his love." It's also new, as new as a promise made and a promise kept, as new as the "truth that sets us free."

Notes

Chapter 1, "What's Your Point?"

1. See Chapter 3, note 2, for a fuller discussion of the way words, sentences, and paragraphs have different levels of meaning, and how they combine to form large unities.

2. You may want to read Chapter 9 for additional insight into my intentions. Since this book is not a detective mystery, you need not fear spoiling it for yourself by knowing still more about the "end from the beginning."

Chapter 2, "But You Promised!"

1. I agree with W. D. Ross, who states that promise-keeping is a self-evident—or what he terms a *prima facie*—duty. To make a promise is to "create a moral claim on us in someone else" (W. D. Ross, *The Right and the Good*, Clarendon, 1930). If that seems so obvious to you that you wonder why either Ross or I would bother to say it, then the point has been made.

2. Giving emergency aid is another *prima facie* duty. We experience it as a preemptive claim, no matter what conflicts it may engender due to other important commitments. We hear a lot nowadays about the riskiness of the Good Samaritan role. You can even take out insurance in case you are sued by the one you try to help. There are highly publicized instances of persons refusing to aid someone in distress. The fact that such instances make the headlines signals more than journalistic sensationalism. We are offended. An implicit promise has been broken: i.e., to give aid when it is needed and when we are in a position to give it.

3. There are excellent resources for further study of the biblical understandings of *shalom*. I would place high on the list Johannes Pedersen, *Israel, Its Life and Culture*. I–II, (1926), pp. 263ff. He is

particularly helpful in describing the close connection between peace and covenant in the "common life of souls." He writes: "One is born of a covenant and into a covenant, and wherever one moves in life, one makes a covenant or acts on the basis of the already existing covenant. If everything that comes under the name of covenant were dissolved, existence would fall to pieces, for no soul can live an isolated life."

You may also wish to consult an earlier article of mine in which I discuss covenant in relation to the theme of election. "The Church: Its Nature and Function," *Brethren Life and Thought,* 6 (Summer, 1961) #3.

4. See John Rawls, "Two Concepts of Rules," *Philosophical Review,* 64 (1955): 2–32. Rawls distinguishes between a "summary" and a "practice" view of rules. In a summary view guidelines drawn from past experience allow us to anticipate future consequences, disciplined by the utilitarian criterion. The goodness of a deed is determined by what's best for the largest number. In a practice view the rules are more than guides for achieving desired outcomes. They define the practice. The rightness of an action results from its conformity to duty.

Rawls illustrated the practice view by the game of baseball. One can throw a rounded object, run, and swing an elongated piece of wood. But you must presuppose the practice, of the game, before you can balk, steal a base, strike out, or hit a home run. If a batter were to ask to have four strikes it would be taken as a joke, or as a request for information about the rules. If the batter persisted, it would be assumed that the person is unable to understand the nature of the game. Where the practice precedes the rules, as in the game of baseball, rules are not merely guides to what is best for the largest number. The rules are interior to, and actually specify the practice. Changing the rules is to change the essentials of the game.

We may relate Rawls' distinction to biblical themes. Covenant understandings developed with Israel over the period of time and on the basis of reflective experience. Therefore one cannot eliminate all elements of a summary view of rules from the Scriptures, where rules are perceived as guides to future action based on past learnings. But essentially covenant has the status of a practice where the rules precede particular cases, for the practice is grounded in God's eternal purpose. As a result, the rules are often presented in an apodictic, or unqualified tone as in the Ten Commandments. To try to rewrite the Ten Commandments for our convenience would demonstrate that we have not grasped the true nature of God's covenant.

5. The debate between a type of ethical reasoning that features utilitarian considerations (teleological) and a type emphasizing un-

qualified obligations (deontological) was not a preoccupation of the biblical writers. They preferred instead to retell, and to call for fitting responses to the story of God's purposes and gracious actions.

H. Richard Niebuhr describes distinctive ethical tendencies in the Bible with the aid of such "root metaphors" as "responsibility" and "fittingness," or what he terms a "fittingness" (cateontological) type of ethical reasoning. "See *The Responsible Self,* Harper, 1963).

Among writings currently helping us to understand how the Bible provides a story or narrative context for ethical and theological thought and fitting life style responses consult: Stanley Hauerwas, *A Community of Character* (University of Notre Dame, 1981); Michael Goldberg, *Theology and Narrative: A Critical Introduction* (Abingdon, 1982); Gabriel Fackre, "Narrative Theology: An Overview," *Interpretation 37* (October, 1983) pp. 340–52; George Lindbeck, *The Nature of Doctrine: Religion in a Post-Liberal Age* (Westminster, 1984); Gabriel Fackre, *The Christian Story* (Eerdmans, 1984); Stanley Hauerwas and William H. Willimon, "Embarrassed by God's Presence," *The Christian Century,* January 30, 1985.

6. Warren F. Groff, "The Sixth Commandment: Its Significance for the Christian as Citizen and for the Statesman," *Brethren Life and Thought,* 6 (Winter 1961).

7. Søren Kierkegaard calls the radical challenge to common sense, promise, obligation and morality "a teleological suspension of the ethical" in *Fear and Trembling,* translated by Walter Lowrie (Princeton, 1942).

Chapter 3, "What's your name?"

1. Our knowledge of each other as persons raises some important issues. Writers such as Martin Buber and G. H. Mead call attention to the way we become an "I" in relation to a "thou"; we become a "self" in relation to the "other." We use terms like kinship and empathy to suggest in close identification between persons when one feels the pain of the other whose face is contorted in grief. An infant often cries spontaneously when someone else cries. There is directness in our knowledge of other persons. That directness is mediated by words, facial features, bodily gestures, which somehow enable us to reconstruct the inner consciousness of the one who is external to us. We experience ourselves and others as unified wholes. The name is central in this whole process. In naming and being named a unitary awareness emerges.

For additional reading I recommend: Gordon D. Kaufman, *Relativism, Knowledge, and Faith* (University of Chicago, 1960). Through Kaufman's succinct statement you will also have access to contributions of such writers as Wilhelm Dilthey, G. H. Mead, and R. G. Collingwood.

Another resource is John Macmurray, *The Self as Agent* (Faber, 1959), especially Chapter V.

2. Language is a collection of words which signify particular objects. Such words are caught up in sentences where word order itself adds a level of meaning. Jerome S. Bruner illustrates how a sentence means more than the particular words it contains. Suppose you give children the following sentences: "The man ate his lunch." "A lady wore my hat." "This doctor broke a bottle." "My son drove our car." The children soon discover that so long as they pick words in proper sequence something "sensible" remains even if you devise a silly mixture. "My doctor wore a car" or "A lady ate a bottle" is at least not "crazy" like "Man the lunch his ate" (referred to in Herbert W. Richardson, "Three Myths of Transcendence," *Transcendence.* ed., Herbert W. Richardson and Donald R. Cutler, Beacon, 1971, p. 106).

Meaning at the level of paragraphs and stories goes beyond words and sentences. Such units are caught up in a still larger totality. Grasping that totality, or experiencing it as image, requires that we perform the typical fourth grade exercise of assigning an appropriate title. A name is such a title, first bestowed by parents, but increasingly made one's own through life's unfolding.

Richardson summarizes a widely accepted distinction between images and signs: "Signs symbolize individuals; images symbolize wholes. Signs communicate by denotation, images by evocation. Signs are the means for communicating observation, images for communicating feeling experiences. Signs are external to the realities they signify (just as an observer is external to the object he observes); hence signs are conventional and replaceable. Images, on the other hand, participate in the reality they express (just as the subject participates in a whole by feeling); hence images are irreplaceable" *ibid.*, p. 102).

The name is a story image. With its aid we experience ourselves, and others experience us, as living wholes, as active and purposeful. The name invites movement from the position of an external observer to a participative relationship. A name is not simply a name—it is the reality it signifies. Through our names we introduce ourselves, and become present—even vulnerable—to one another.

For a discussion of the meaning of "symbol" in contrast to "sign" read Paul Tillich, *Dynamics of Faith* (Harper, 1957), pp. 41-54.

3. The centrality of the name Jesus Christ for New Testament witnesses is discussed by Karl Barth, *Church Dogmatics,* Volume IV, Part Two, translated by G.W. Bromiley (Ediburgh, 1958), pp. 46ff. and 107ff.

Chapter 4, "Just Because!"

1. When others fail to see what seems so clear to us, how often do we respond to the persistent "why?"—seventy-times-seven? When is "just because" evasive? Isn't it expected that we "give reasons" for our likes and dislikes, and especially for our basic beliefs?

The issue posed for the life of faith is how do we "give reasons" for our deepest convictions and commitments? You may wish to puruse this question with the aid of supplementary readings. H. Richard Niebuhr speaks of revelation as the "story of our life," as encouraging a level of sharing that draws upon "reasons of the heart" (using language from Pascal). He states that revelation is "that special occasion by means of which all the occasions of personal and common life become intelligible . . . it illuminates other events and enables us to understand them . . . it does mean an event in our history which brings rationality and wholeness into the confused joys and sorrows of personal existence and allows us to discern order in the brawl of communal histories. Such revelation is no substitute for reasons; the illumination it supplies does not excuse the mind from labor; but it does give to that mind the impulsion and the first principles it requires if it is to be able to do its proper work" *The Meaning of Revelation* (Macmillan, 1946), p. 109. Notice how references to "light" and "illumination" recur in Niebuhr's thought about revelation. Picking up an observation in my chapter, revelation has to do with "how we see all that we see."

Also consult H. Richard Niebuhr, *The Responsible Self* (Harper, 1963), Appendix A. He deals with "root-metaphors" and their bearing on moral activity. ". . . in Christian life Jesus Christ is a symbolic form with the aid of which men tell each other what life and death, God and man, are *like;* but even more he is a form which they employ as an *a priori,* an image, a scheme or pattern in the mind which gives form and meaning to their experience" (p. 154).

I have developed this thought of Jesus Christ as an historical *a priori* in *Christ the Hope of the Future: Signals of a Promised Humanity* (Eerdmans, 1971).

2. "Reasons of the heart" lend themselves to personal testimony, to confessional recital. The focus of that recital is upon those meanings and images which inform one's personal history, and which point beyond themselves toward the larger story of God's purpose in Jesus Christ. A resource from the broader heritage is Augustine, *The Confessions.*

For reflections on commitments and convictions and the difficulties in giving adequate reasons for them, see H. Richard Niebuhr, *The Meaning of Revelation* (Macmillan, 1946).

3. These "just because" affirmations about Christ presuppose some basic theological judgments on my part:

(1) Jesus Christ precedes our experience as a life-shaping image.

(2) Since that image relates us to a specific person from the past his life and work are open to the disciplined observations of the historian. The security of faith does not require that dogmatic considerations be intruded as defensive limits on research.

(3) Truth is not accessible only to the dispassionate researcher whose posture is that of subject (the one who does the knowing) standing at arm's length from the object (what is known). Participation and the passionate investments of the believer are also avenues to truth. In story time the distance of the one doing the knowing (subject) from what one knows (object) is overcome. We "stand within" events and meanings which intersect with, and are becoming "our story."

(4) Totalities such as a story (images) have their own claim to truth and significance, even though they cannot be perceived by observation or be made known by direct indication; even though they are not identical with their parts, any more than paragraphs are exhausted by their words and sentences.

(5) One does not move directly from the parts to the whole. Acceptance of a story title invites a creative response. Similarly, we do not move directly from history to faith, for faith is a voluntary commitment. It is obedience to the central story line of God's purpose.

If you wish further amplification of the theological reasoning behind these judgments see Warren F. Groff and Donald E. Miller, *The Shaping of Modern Christian Thought* (World, 1968), Parts I & III. Also consult my *Christ the Hope of the Future.*

Chapter 5; "You Ought to Be Ashamed!"

1. Freedom has the double movement which the Apostle Paul reflects when he responds to the Corinthians on the issue of food offered to idols. " . . . We know that 'an idol has no real existence,' and that 'there is no God but one.' . . . However, not all possess this knowledge. But some, through being hitherto accustomed to idols, eat food as really offered to an idol; and their conscience, being weak, is defiled. . . . Therefore, if food is a cause of my brother's falling, I will never eat meat, lest I cause my brother to fall" (1 Corinthians 8:4b, 7, 13).

Martin Luther captures the same movements and countermovements that flow through the life of freedom when he reminds us that the Christian is "a perfectly free lord of all, subject to none," and is "a perfectly dutiful servant of all, subject to all" (*A Treatise on Christian Liberty*).

2. Upon reflection, the Groffs are more Calvinistic than I first thought in their attitudes toward the possible legitimacy of an "ought," or the "law." In this "I'm O.K., you're O.K." era we are being reminded that an oppressive sense of obligation, with its self-depreciating shame, is debilitating. But if freedom is escaping *from* a harsh, commanding "ought" imposed from the outside, it is also being released *for* life in covenant with its deeply interior "ought" and rules of covenantal "practice." (See above, Chapter 2, note 4.)

Read John Calvin, *Institutes of the Christian Religion,* Book II, Chapter VII. Calvin identifies three uses of law: (1) "The law is a kind of mirror. As in a mirror we discover any stains upon our face, so in the Law we behold, first, our impotence; then, in consequence of it, our iniquity; and, finally, the curse, as the consequence of both." (2) "The second office of the Law is, by means of its fearful denunciations and the consequent dread of punishment, to curb those who, unless forced, have no regard for rectitude and justice." (3) "The third use of the Law (being also the principal use, and more closely connected with its proper end) has respect to believers in whose hearts the Spirit of God already flourishes and reigns . . . the doctrine of the Law has not been infringed by Christ, but remains, that, by teaching, admonishing, rebuking, and correcting, it may fit and prepare us for every good work" (paragraphs 7, 10, 12, 14).

There are differences of accent between Luther and Calvin on this issue. Luther admits that the law is necessary to restrain the wicked, and that its teachings and exhortations are vital for those who abuse the freedom of faith, or confuse freedom with license. But for the believer, insofar as the believer truly stands in the righteousness of faith he receives as God's pure gift of grace, the law is not necessary. The law itself, and not merely its curse, is abrogated.

Chapter 6: "It's All Your Fault!"

1. It was B. Davie Napier who first called my attention to the recurrent pattern in Old Testament stories of promising beginnings that are then marred by seduction and betrayal, with bitter consequences—"expulsion from the garden"—for individuals like Saul and David and for the people as a whole. Materials from lectures I first heard while a student of his at Yale Divinity School are available in *From Faith to Faith,* (Harper, 1955).

2, A basic theological issue, and one I do not pretend to have explored fully in this chapter, is what happens to our view of God if the devil is too glibly eliminated from the story. I suppose you might turn that question around and ask what the implications are for God's unity if we take the demonic quite seriously. Does the devil introduce an unfortunate dualism into our thinking? We must not ignore the clear biblical teaching about the oneness of God and the essential goodness of his creation.

We cope with unexplained suffering, tragedy, deception. Do we trace all suffering back to God? That places a dualism within God himself. Do we attribute it to "fate?" That hardly adds much clarity. Do we interpret it as retribution? What about the suffering persons clearly do not deserve? Do we account for deception and its disastrous outworkings on the basis of human sinfulness which then gets institutionalized and perpetuated with cumulative power? See Walter Rauschenbusch, *A Theology for the Social Gospel,* (Macmillan, 1917). This is an important perspective, but it still leaves aspects of the problem untouched. Is the devil the way God himself appears to us, or God in his judgment and wrath, in face of our proud rebellion? That has the advantage of preserving God's unity but may again miss the depth of the struggle.

I have said in this chapter that one of the meanings symbolized by the devil is the sheer mystery of the deception that enters and rips its way through the story. The Scriptures do not give an explanation of the presence of evil. If we try to evade our personal responsibility by blaming the devil rather than acknowledging our complicity in it all, that is exposed as one basic form of the devil's deception. We struggle against "principalities and powers," against whom Christ's battle is fought and the victory is won. In the text of the chapter, I develop the thesis that "if the devil goes, compassion goes." Now we can see that "if the devil goes, the full magnitude of Christ's victory goes." For a fuller discussion of Christ's atoning work see Gustaf Aulen, *Christus Victor.*

Just how pervasive and difficult are the issues posed by suffering and tragedy is evidenced by the popularity of the book by Harold S. Kushner, *When Bad Things Happen to Good People* (Avon, 1981).

Chapter 7, "Be Good! Stay Out of Trouble!"

1. To what extent was Jesus a revolutionary, or at least closely identified with such groups and causes? That question is being discussed extensively nowadays. The portrait I carry of Jesus is that he was a constant threat to the establishment. However, he did not confront the state with the raw power of a revolutionary who seeks to accomplish a righteous "end" even by violent "means." The revolutionary is convinced that "structural violence" is already part of the status quo. Jesus undoubtedly shared such concerns, but he did not go all the way with the Zealots of his day. Nor did he join the Essenes and withdraw from the political struggle. His life-style was the voluntary vulnerability of the servant. The troublemaking of the servant places that one at the juncture between God's purpose and all that rebelliously opposes what God intends. There the battle is intense, and may issue in suffering, even death on the cross.

A resource for further study is John Howard Yoder, *The Politics of Jesus* (Eerdmans, 1972).

2. Kermit Eby a Brethren educator and labor leader came to a similar conclusion some time before I did. I recall hearing him say that he was an adult before he realized that—the family admonitions notwithstanding—it is impossible to "Be good!" (as Christ establishes the norm for goodness) and to "Stay out of trouble!" See his *For Brethren Only* (Brethren Press, 1958), but don't believe the title. It's not really "for Brethren only!"

Chapter 8, "Say Thank You!"

1. This chapter raises the issue of the way we view symbolic activities. Language functions as symbol. Language is not simply verbal. It includes whatever expresses and communicates meanings between persons: words, exclamation, gestures, ritual—spontaneous and formalized. Language participates in the very meaning it expresses.

As I write I am surrounded by a variety of household noises. Usually my concentration is such that I screen out most of them. But just this moment I become aware of a sweeper being used to clean the rug in the living room. Obviously the noise was there for some time in the background. But by the explicit thought that surfaces within me, "That sweeper is loud!" and by getting up to close the study door, I experience the "noise" being expressed in my interior monolog and nonverbal gesture. When I name something I call it to my attention. I become conscious of it by paying attention to it.

Parents sense the importance of language as a symbolic activity when they encourage the child to say the words—"Say thank you!" In the church and in our households it is most fitting that we be admonished to "Say our prayers!"—whether in the mood of praise, petition, penitence, or intercession. Even more inclusively to repeat a central concern of this book as a whole, we do well to exhort one another to "Tell the story!" for language—in all forms—is an ordinance, a vehicle, for experiencing what we express.

2. I am concerned that we sometimes neglect Paul's insights about justification, about God's righteousness as an action on our behalf. As a result, we lose the joy of discipleship. We struggle against permissiveness and uncritical acculturation in the church. So I am not here mounting one more attack against the threat of legalism. I doubt whether legalism is that serious a problem today. But the answer to the heresy of mistaking license for Christian freedom is not a view of discipleship which must "prove itself" through works. Paul reminds us that we are to "stand fast" in the freedom to which Christ has called us, the freedom of faith, of trust and gratitude, which "works itself out through love."

Chapter 9, "Tell Me a Story!"

1. For additional reflections on the importance of corporate memory in presenting us with the story of God's purpose consult: R. M. Hare, "Philosophical Discoveries," in Richard Rorty (ed.), *The Linguistic Turn* (The University of Chicago Press, 1967); H. L. Harrod, "Christ as Predecessor and Contemporary" *Journal of the American Academy of Religion*, XLIV (June 1976).

2. Elie Wiesel, *The Gates of the Forest* (Avon, 1973), pp. 6, 9, 10.

3. Martin E. Marty, *The Fire We Can Light* (Doubleday, 1974). Here Marty describes the shape of American religion. He concentrates on those persons and groups who no longer "content themselves with words about experience instead of having the experience itself."

4. The quote is from my paraphrase found above. Consult Harvey Cox, *The Seduction of the Spirit: The Use and Misuse of Peo-*

ple's Religion (Simon & Schuster, 1974, who is also addressing the problem of the story's seduction.

5. Sam Keen, *To a Dancing God* (Harper, 1970), p. 86. Keen features individual biography as a theological starting point since the "events of our own personal lives tell a story of promise and fulfillment and give a testimony to the presence of a power within human history which makes for wholeness and and freedom."

Bibliography

Achtemeier, Paul. *The Inspiration of Scripture.* Philadelphia: Westminster Press, 1980.

Barbour, Ian. *Myths, Models and Paradigms.* New York: Harper and Row, 1974.

Barr, James. *The Bible in the Modern World.* New York: Harper and Row, 1973.

Barth, Karl. *The Faith of the Church.* Translated with an introduction by Gabriel Vahanian, New York: Meridian Books, 1958 (also *Church Dogmatics,* Volumes I-IV).

Braithwaite, R.B. *An Empiricist's View of the Nature of Religious Belief.* Cambridge: University of Cambridge Press, 1955.

Brown, Dale W. *Biblical Pacifism. A Peace Church Prospective,* Elgin: Brethren Press, 1986.

_____. *Simulations on Brethren History.* Elgin: Brethren Press, 1976.

Buechner, Frederick. *A Room Called Remember.* New York: Harper and Row, 1984.

Childs, Brevard. *Biblical Theology in Crisis.* Philadelphia: Westminster Press, 1970.

Cox, Harvey. *The Seduction of the Spirit: The Use and Misuse of People's Religion.* New York: Simon & Schuster, 1973.

Crossan, John Dominic. *The Dark Interval: Towards a Theology of Story.* Niles, Illinois; Argus Communications, 1975.

_____. *Cliffs of Fall: Paradox and Polyvalence in the Parables of Jesus.* New York: Seabury Press, 1980.

Dahl, Nils. *Jesus in the Memory of the Early Church.* Minneapolis: Augsburg, 1976.

Dulles, Avery. *Models of Revelation.* New York: Doubleday, 1983.

Dunne, John. *A Search for God in Time and Memory.* New York: Macmillan, 1969.

Durnbaugh, Donald F. *The Believers' Church.* New York: Macmillan, 1968.

Faus, Nancy Rosenberger. *Singing for Peace.* Carol Stream, Illinois: Hope Publishing, 1986.

Frei, Hans. *The Eclipse of Biblical Narrative.* New Haven, Connecticut: Yale University Press, 1974.

_____. *The Identity of Jesus Christ.* Philadelphia: Fortress Press, 1975.

Gilkey, Langdon. *Reaping the Whirlwind.* New York: Seabury Press, 1976.

Goldberg, Michael. *Theology and Narrative: A Critical Introduction.* Nashville: Abingdon Press, 1982.

Groff, Warren F. and Miller, Donald E. *The Shaping of Modern Christian Thought.* New York: World Publishing, 1968.

Groff, Warren F. *Christ the Hope of the Future.* Grand Rapids, Michigan, Eerdmans, 1971.

_____. *Prayer: God's Time and Ours.* Elgin, Illinois: Brethren Press, 1984.

Gustafson, James M. *Christ and the Moral Life.* New York: Harper and Row, 1968.

Hartt, Julian. *A Christian Critique of American Culture.* New York: Harper and Row, 1967.

Harvey, Van Austin. *The Historian and the Believer.* New York: Macmillan, 1966.

Hauerwas, Stanley. *A Community of Character.* Notre Dame, Indiana: University of Notre Dame Press, 1981.

_____. *The Peaceable Kingdom.* Notre Dame, Indiana: University of Notre Dame Press, 1983.

Hauerwas, Stanley, with Richard Bondi and David B. Burrell. *Truthfulness and Tragedy: Further Investigations in Christian Ethics.* Notre Dame, Indiana: University of Notre Dame Press, 1977.

Haughton, Rosemary. *The Transformation of Man.* London: Geoffrey Chapman, 1967.

Kaufman, Gordon D. *Systematic Theology: A Historicist Perspective.* New York: Charles Scribner's Son, 1968.

Keck, Leander. *A Future for the Historical Jesus.* Nashville: Abingdon Press, 1971.

Keen, Sam. *To a Dancing God.* New York: Harper and Row, 1970.

Kelsey, David. *The Uses of Scriptures in Recent Theology.* Philadelphia: Fortress Press, 1975.

Kermode, Frank. *The Genesis of Secrecy: On the Interpretation of Narrative.* Cambridge, Massachusetts: Harvard University Press, 1979.

MacIntyre, Alasdair. *After Virtue*. Second ed. Notre Dame: University of Notre Dame Press, 1984.

Marty, Martin E. *The Fire We Can Light*. New York: Doubleday, 1974.

McClendon, James Wm., Jr. *Biography as Theology*. Nashville: Abingdon Press, 1974.

_____. *Ethics: Systematic Theology,* Volume I. Nashville: Abingdon Press, 1986.

Miller, Donald E., and Snyder, Graydon F., and Neff, Robert W. *Using Biblical Simulations*. Valley Forge, Pennsylvania: Judson Press, 1973-75.

Miller, Donald E. and Poling, James N. *Foundations for a Practical Theology of Ministry*. Nashville: Abingdon Press, 1985.

Niebuhr, H. Richard. *The Meaning of Revelation*. New York: Macmillan, 1946.

_____. *The Responsible Self.* New York: Harper and Row, 1963.

Pannenberg, Wolfhart. *Jesus—God and Man*. Philadelphia: Westminster Press, 1968.

Ramsey, Ian T. *Religious Language*. London: SCM Press, 1957.

Richardson, Herbert W. And Cutler, Donald R. (eds.). *Transcendence*. Boston: Beacon Press, 1969.

Roop, Eugene F. *Living the Biblical Story*. Nashville: Abingdon Press, 1979.

Sayers, Dorothy L. *The Mind of the Maker*. New York: Meridian Books, 1956.

Scott, Jr., Nathan K. *The Tragic Vision and the Christian Faith*. New York: Association Press, 1957.

Sittler, Joseph. *Grace Notes and Other Fragments*. Philadelphia: Fortress Press, 1981.

Snyder, Graydon F. *Ante Pacem: Archaeological Evidence of Church Life Before Constantine*. Macon, Georgia: Mercer,1985.

TeSelle, Sallie McFague. *Speaking in Parables*. Philadelphia: Fortress Press, 1975.

Tilley, Terrence W. *Talking of God: An Introduction to Philosophical Analysis of Religious Language*. New York: Paulist Press, 1978.

_____. *Story Theology.* Wilmington, Delaware: Michael Glazier, 1985.

Tillich, Paul. *Dynamics of Faith*. New York: Harper, 1957 (also *Systematic Theology,* Volumes 1-3).

Tracy, David. *The Analogical Imagination*. New York: Crossroads, 1981.

Wagner, Murray L. *Petr Chĕlcichý: A Radical Separatist in Hussite Bohemia.* Foreword by Jerold K. Zeman. Scottsdale, Pennsylvania: Herald Press, 1983.

Wiesel, Elie. Translated from the French by Frances Frenaye. *The Gates of the Forest.* New York: Holt, Rinehart and Winston, fourth printing (Bard Edition) 1972.

Wiggins, James B., ed. *Religion as Story.* New York: Harper and Row, 1975.

William H. Willimon. *The Service of God.* Nashville: Abingdon Press, 1983.

Yoder, John Howard. *The Politics of Jesus.* Grand Rapids, Michigan: Eerdmans, 1972.